WINTE

winter trails ™
trails

Montana

The Best Cross-Country Ski
& Snowshoe Trails

by
JEAN ARTHUR

The
Globe
Pequot
Press

GUILFORD, CONNECTICUT

Copyright © 2001 by The Globe Pequot Press

Winter Trails is a trademark of The Globe Pequot Press.

Cover photographs: Top photo by Hubert Schriebl; bottom photo courtesy Tubbs Snowshoe Company, Stowe, Vermont
Cover and interior design: Nancy Freeborn
Trail Maps created by Equator Graphics © The Globe Pequot Press
All interior photographs © Jean Arthur, with the exception of photos on page 125 (© Reid Sanders) and page 151 (courtesy B Bar Guest Ranch)

Library of Congress Cataloging-in-Publication Data

Arthur, Jean, 1960-
    Winter trails. Montana : the best cross-country ski & snowshoe trails / by Jean Arthur.— 1st ed.
        p. cm. — (Winter trails series)
    ISBN 0–7627–0730-5
        1. Cross-country skiing—Montana—Guidebooks. 2. Snowshoes and snowshoeing—Montana—Guidebooks. 3. Cross-country ski trails—Montana—Guidebooks. 4. Montana—Guidebooks. I. Title. II. Series.

GV854.5.M9 A79 2000
917.8604'34—dc21

                                                        00–057680

Manufactured in the United States of America
First Edition/First Printing

Acknowledgments

Many people and organizations helped in the creation of *Winter Trails: Montana.* As you experience these trails, don't forget to thank the local skiers, their organizations, and the state and federal agencies and their employees for the wonderful trail systems, grooming, maintenance, and maps.

A special thanks to the following people: Lynn, Gretchen, and Bridger Sellegren; Laura Strong; Rhonda Fitzgerald; Rusty Wells; Laura Nugent; Cris Coughlin; Dave Streeter; Dee Blank; Becky Smith-Powell; Ed Madej; Peter Hale; Peter Kurtz; Jonathan Wiesel; Reid Sanders; Mike Bryers; Lyle Schultze; Mike Dye; Ranger Tim Fisher; Kim Hoberecht; Greg and Susie Rice; Lynn Carey; Dick Fichtler; Kimberly Mitman; John Wulf; Tommy Cockerham III; Karen Kohut; Jean MacInnes; and Bill Blackford.

Another thank you goes to the following: Glacier Nordic Club; Outback Ski Shack; Madshus; Alfa; Rottefella; Patagonia; Yoko Gloves; Cherokee Personal Radios; Smith Optics; SmartWool; SpringBrook Manufacturing; Backcountry Access, Inc.; Travel Montana; Jackson Hot Springs Lodge; Yellowstone Alpen Guides; Beartooth Mountain Guides; West Yellowstone Conference Hotel; Lone Mountain Ranch; Mountain Meadows Guest Ranch; Cooke City Bike Shack; Glacier Park Ski Guides; Lone Mountain Ranch; Mountain Meadows Guest Ranch; North Fork Hostel, Cabins and Square Peg Ranch; Izaak Walton Inn; and the personnel from the U.S. Forest Service, the Bureau of Land Management, and the U.S. Park Service who so generously offered their time and expertise.

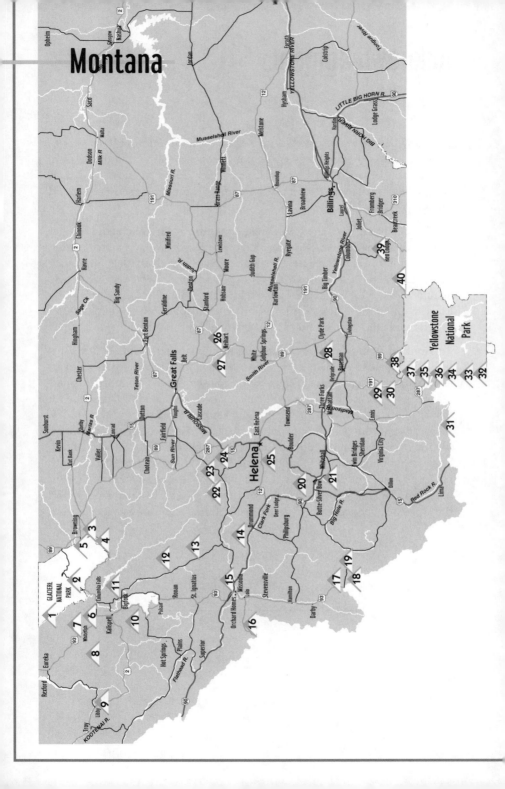

Montana

Contents

Introduction

Montana is a mountainous state that provides hundreds of miles of ski terrain that is locked in winter from late October into May. The forty trails and trail systems detailed here offer a variety of ski and snowshoe terrain—from tidy, groomed tracks to experts-only backcountry. Hundreds of other ski and snowshoe opportunities exist in Montana's remote mountains.

There is an element of danger inherent in any winter activity in the mountains. Backcountry visitors must be prepared to deal with severe winter weather, avalanches, wildlife, and equipment problems. Preparedness, self-reliance, fitness, and safety are the keys to enjoying Montana's backcountry in the winter.

While traveling Montana's trails, visitors are often amazed at the pristine wilderness. While fewer than 900,000 people live in Montana, the state in 1999 hosted some 9.4 million visitors, of whom 1.7 million were winter guests. To keep the trails pristine, visitors must participate in a "pack in, pack out" travel ethic. Whatever is brought into the wild should be carried back out, whether it's an apple core or broken equipment. Your help is needed to keep Montana a wild place for your next visit.

Trail Selections and Ratings

The trails highlighted in this book are among the favorites of local skiers and snowshoers. Offered here is a mix of groomed resort trail systems, ungroomed routes on summer hiking trails, and off-piste backcountry ascents and descents. If you're traveling a long distance to ski or snowshoe Montana's trails, consider spending at least one day acclimatizing to the elevation and the weather. For the most part, Montana's trails are not in the highest peaks of the Rocky Mountains. However, if you're traveling from sea level, remember that the air is thinner at these elevations and that altitude sickness may be a concern.

Dogs are not allowed on most of these trails. However, some ski and snowshoe paths, mostly on U.S. Forest Service roads that are snow-covered in winter and impassable to cars and trucks, are open to dogs traveling with their owners. Check locally for specific trail regulations before starting out with dogs.

Within each chapter, trail designations include an estimation of difficulty. Easiest, more difficult, most difficult, and expert trail indicators assist visitors in finding a trail, determining a distance, and evaluating equipment needs. The *easiest* trails are suitable for novice skiers and snowshoers. Gentle terrain presents little or no altitude loss/gain. People new to skiing should take a ski lesson before heading into the backcountry. Several of the guest ranches and Nordic centers listed in this book offer ski lessons by certified ski instructors.

More difficult trails offer more challenging terrain and longer distances than beginner routes. These intermediate trails are suitable for skiers and snowshoers who have some trail experience, are moderately fit, and can comfortably ski or snowshoe a half day or more. You should be able to read maps, handle a variety of terrain and snow conditions, and be comfortable climbing and descending hills.

Most difficult trails challenge even the most fit athletes, yet these trails can be skied or snowshoed using light backcountry gear with edges on skis or cleats on snowshoes. Advanced backcountry and winter survival skills and equipment are necessary.

Expert routes place adventurers in avalanche-prone regions where route-finding skills are required. Expert terrain is generally very steep, remote, mountainous, and beautiful. Skiers and snowshoers must be competent backcountry winter travelers with a thorough knowledge of avalanche danger and emergency response techniques. They should also have the ability to make telemark or alpine ski turns or downhill snowshoe maneuvers.

Numerous avalanche advisory centers and outdoor schools across the United States and Canada offer avalanche seminars to help backcountry adventurers understand the dynamics and dangers of snow packs. Before venturing into the backcountry, take an avalanche course. If a course is not available, hire a guide.

Equipment and Survival Gear

Ski and snowshoe equipment evolves every year with lighter, faster, and stronger materials, giving the skier and snowshoer the advantage of technology while enjoying the solitude of the trails. While older skis and snowshoes might be adequate, beware of bindings that may be weak from wear. Test all equipment before hitting the trails. Consider what would happen if you suffered a serious equipment breakdown 10 miles out on the trail. Carry spare equipment, such as an extra pole basket and a repair kit that includes duct tape.

Older bindings, such as the three-pin variety, can fatigue with time and use. Consider Rottefella's new BC binding for backcountry ski travel. These beefy bindings have a wide foot plate that offers extra stability, especially when climbing side hills or telemarking untracked terrain.

I have had great success with the Rottefella bindings on Madshus skis with Alfa's BC Boots. The lug sole offers rugged stability off the skis as well as comfort on them. Alfa's backcountry boots and track boots are the warmest and most comfortable I've found.

Backcountry skis, such as the Madshus Voss, equipped with a ¾ steel edge and Multigrip-patterned base, combine flexibility and light weight. They are ruggedly trustworthy. Madshus and Rottefella classic and skate equipment are my choices for groomed trails because of their light and responsive action. Skiers on machine-groomed flat and rolling terrain will want skis with a wax-free base, like Madshus's Trondheim Multigrip, or skis that use kick wax, such as Madshus's Lillehammer. Comparable skis come from Atomic, Karhu, and Fischer.

Several snowshoe manufacturers offer an extensive line of high-tech snowshoes, such as Little Bears, Tubbs, and Atlas. SpringBrook Manufacturing's Little Bear snowshoes for kids are an inexpensive and nearly indestructible line of snowshoes in bright colors and different sizes. Their adult Saguache snowshoes offer the flexibility of high-tech, light-weight materials and a sturdy platform for climbing and traversing. Some snowshoers use one or two ski poles for stability.

Anyone who has spent a cold, wet day on the trails, far from the trailhead and a warm hearth, appreciates the new fabrics available for outdoor wear. I find that the more clothing I try, the more often I go back to certain brands that I trust, such as Patagonia for the well-made Capilene under layers, fleece, and storm coat. I've bought less expensive brands only to be disappointed with poor quality, blown-out zippers, and lack of pockets.

The same goes for kids' outdoor gear. The cheaper the clothing, the less likely the kids will stay warm and dry. Patagonia's line of kids' winter clothing includes the same quality of under and outerwear as the adult versions.

I get warm when track skiing. I've found a new ski pant made from a fabric called SP3 that is more than a stretch pant. The XC Pant made by SportHill is windproof and dries quickly. Garments made of SP3 can be washed and hung to dry overnight during lightweight travel.

Wool's timeless quality for weight and warmth shines with products like Smart Wool's ski socks, which come in a variety of thicknesses. The socks' ability to wick away dampness from the inner layer and absorb dampness in the outer layer helps to keep your feet warm all day. Smart Wool also makes an itchless wool turtleneck that is warm and doesn't retain odors. Smart Wool's best feature is that all the wool products are machine-washable and -dryable.

Savvy backcountry travelers know to carry an extra pair of gloves or mittens. Gloves that get sweaty and damp on an ascent will be cold on the descent. I've found Yoko gloves, made in Finland, to be the warmest cross-country ski gloves on the market. Yoko uses Thermo Gore Windstopper in its extreme cold weather gloves, resulting in warm hands in near-zero temperatures.

Another outstanding product for the backcountry is the Smith Optics line of Sliders sunglasses. These specs come with three different lenses for different lighting situations. If the trail starts out sunny, use the sienna brown lens. Late afternoon and the light gets flat, slide out the sienna brown and slide in the gold lite or yellow lenses, which bring out terrain detail in flat light. Sliders come in several styles, and replacement lenses are available in additional colors, such as brown polarized, optimal for high-altitude travel on snow.

Of course all the extra clothing, extra hat, extra gloves, and food and emergency gear are carried in a backpack. Be sure to use a pack that fits not only your body size but the use to which you're going to put it. Dana Designs, for example, makes everything from day packs to expedition packs that adjust for a remarkably comfortable fit using the ArcFlex Frame System. Dana Design's Slider day pack is popular with the snowboard crowd. The snowboard cinches onto the back of the pack while climbing with snowshoes. Snowshoes fit inside or outside of the Slider pack when you're shredding downhill. Dana Design's Bomb Pack adjusts for body frame size. When properly fit, the Bomb Pack comfortably carries enough food and gear for a long day trip or even an overnight into a hut. For expeditions, Dana Design's Alpine AV pack carries the big load of backcountry necessities.

Skiers planning to climb for steep powder turns need safety and climbing equipment for success. Climbing skins, which are made from a synthetic, fur-like fabric, attach to the bottom of skis to make it possible to climb steep terrain. Once on the mountain top, the climbing skins are carefully folded, sticky side to sticky, and placed in a backpack.

Avalanche experts suggest carrying—and knowing how to use—an avalanche transceiver, a lightweight snow shovel, probe poles, a snow saw, an inclinometer, and a first-aid kit. Back Country Access sells an easy-to-use avalanche locator beacon/transceiver called the Tracker. The Tracker is a digital avalanche beacon that eliminates the traditional grid search procedure and instead pinpoints a buried victim. Remember that for transceivers to work, they must be turned on, and every member of a party must wear his or her own unit.

Two-way sport radios are handy when traveling the trails with skiers or snowshoers who are moving at different speeds. Cherokee Electronics'

FR-465 radios provide local communications in the backcountry. Although Cherokee says the radios are limited to about 2 miles line-of-sight for communicating, I've been able to contact ski partners up to 5 miles away, from mountain peak to valley bottom, with an open line of sight.

Prior to any trip, adventurers should check all equipment to see that it is in working order and that all the pieces are together.

Trip Planning and Trail Safety

Montana's snowy wilds invite skiers and snowshoers to luxuriously remote spots. With proper planning, these trips are enjoyable and memorable. The maps and trail descriptions included in this book are to be used as guides. Note that trails can change from year to year as a result of land-steward decisions, snow coverage, weather, and other events. Check locally with outdoor shops or Forest Service, Bureau of Land Management, or Park Service offices regarding trail conditions and changes. Maps and information on trail conditions are available at many trailheads. General Montana travel information can be found at www.visit.com or (800) 847–4868.

Travelers should carry detailed maps and a compass, and should always check avalanche information. The latest navigational tool is the Global Positioning System (GPS) receiver, a hand-held device that will provide precise latitude and longitude coordinates. Properly used in conjunction with a good map, GPS receivers are superb navigational tools, but remember that terrain and foliage in some backcountry areas can interfere with their performance.

In some Montana ski regions, such as Glacier and Yellowstone National Parks, skilled backcountry guide services are available. Guides know the trails, the terrain, dangers, and trail conditions, and also can provide a wealth of information about the environment and history of the backcountry.

Montana winter travelers know that there's always a chance of a blizzard or other weather condition that can inhibit travel or close roads. Always carry an emergency kit in your car during the winter. Include a gallon of water, emergency food, sleeping bags, extra winter clothing (especially gloves and hats), and emergency flares. Before driving winter roads, check road conditions at (800) 226–ROAD (7623).

Basic safe-travel tips apply whenever you're planning a trip. Always leave a travel plan and itinerary with someone who will notify search and rescue agencies if you do not return on the appointed day. When you return from the backcountry, don't forget to notify your home contact person to prevent a false search from being launched. Search and rescue operations in Montana are generally activated by a sheriff's office and implemented by volunteers who are taking time away from work and families.

Montana's natives include grizzly bears, which generally hibernate during the winter. However, active grizzly and black bears have been seen in all months of the year. Never approach any bear at any time of year. The Park Service recommends that if you are charged by a bear, do not run or ski away—flight can entice the bear to give chase. People should make themselves look as small as possible, assume the fetal position, cover their heads, and show no aggression toward the animal.

If you are confronted by a mountain lion, try to look as *big* as possible. Throw rocks and sticks at the animal. Hold a backpack or branches over your head to look larger.

Moose and bison can be very dangerous. Slowly back away from them. Approaching them can antagonize these animals and cause them to charge.

Travel over frozen lakes, rivers, and streams is not recommended. Travel on ice is dangerous. If you choose to ski or snowshoe over a frozen body of water, use extreme caution, crossing one person at a time. Never cross dark-colored or slush-covered ice.

Avalanches are a chronic danger in the state. In avalanche country, you should always be equipped with avalanche gear. But the first and best defense against avalanches is knowing how to avoid them. Leeward slopes are usually the most dangerous because of wind-deposited snow that may be unstable and susceptible to slab avalanches. Avoid crossing steep, open slopes. The safest routes are on ridge tops, on the windward sides of mountains, or in trees and away from obvious avalanche chutes.

Several avalanche information centers in Montana offer regional snow conditions. Always check with avalanche centers prior to a trip, or even weekly all winter for a cumulative knowledge of the snow's layering. Note that most of the following avalanche information centers only operate during the snowy months, November through April.

- Cooke City (406) 838–2341
- National Avalanche Center www.csac.org/Bulletins/ or www.avalanche.org/
- Northwest Montana (406) 257–8402 or in Montana (800) 526–5329
- Southwest Montana's Gallatin National Forest Avalanche Center (406) 587–6981; www.mtavalanche.com
- West Yellowstone (406) 646–7912
- West-Central Montana's Missoula Regional Avalanche Advisory (406) 549–4488 or in Montana (800) 281–1030

Backcountry Etiquette

Montanans are known for their friendliness. Please respect traditions, customs, and local ordinances and the local folks will keep smiling. Most winter visitors come to snowmobile, while only a small percentage come to ski or snowshoe. In general, both groups recreate in harmony. Trail etiquette requires that a fast-moving skier or snowmobiler must yield to a trail user moving more slowly.

This book leads skiers into some pristine places, historic sites, and unique settings. Please help preserve Montana's heritage by leaving ghost towns, mining camps, and other historic attractions intact. Take only photographs and leave only ski or snowshoe tracks. Respect rights of property owners by asking permission before entering private land. Pack out trash. Watch wildlife from a distance—for the animals' safety and yours.

A Word About Maps

U.S. Geological Survey maps—topographic maps—form the underlying basis of the trail maps in this book. The U.S. Geological Survey is in the process of converting its topographic maps from feet to meters. Because this is an ongoing project, not every U.S. Geological Survey map has been converted. Therefore, you will find that on some maps in this book, elevations appear in feet while on others they appear in meters. A box on the map tells you if the elevations are in meters.

Key to Icons

cross-country skiing trail

snowshoeing trail

skate skiing (skating) trail

Help Us Keep This Guide Up to Date

Every effort has been made by the author and editors to make this guide as accurate and useful as possible. However, many things can change after a guide is published—new products and information become available, regulations change, techniques evolve, etc.

We would love to hear from you concerning your experiences with this guide and how you feel it could be improved and be kept up to date. While we may not be able to respond to all comments and suggestions, we'll take them to heart and we'll make certain to share them with the author. Please send your comments and suggestions to the following address:

The Globe Pequot Press
Reader Response/Editorial Department
P.O. Box 480
Guilford, CT 06437

Or you may e-mail us at:
editorial@globe-pequot.com

Thanks for your input, and happy travels!

montana

Big Prairie and Bowman Lake

Glacier National Park, Montana

Type of trail:	▬▬ ⬮⬮⬮
Also used by:	Wildlife
Distance:	12 miles/19.2 kilometers
Terrain:	Flat meadows, rolling hills, and steep hills
Trail difficulty:	Easy to more difficult
Surface quality:	Skier-packed
Elevation:	3,600 to 4,040 feet
Food and facilities:	Polebridge, a community of about twenty-five full-time residents, has no electricity. Propane and kerosene lanterns light the nights here. In winter, only the Polebridge Mercantile and the North Fork Hostel are open daily. The Merc's bakery offers excellent baked goods. The Merc also sells snacks, camping supplies, souvenirs, and dry goods. Its hours are limited during the winter. Three blocks south of the Merc on Beaver Drive is the North Fork Hostel, Cabins and Square Peg Ranch. The hostel's cozy lodging includes access to the kitchen. Guests bring their own bedding and food and cook their own meals. Reservations are advised and dogs are welcome, although dogs are not allowed in Glacier National Park backcountry. Columbia Falls, Whitefish, and Kalispell have all services. The Cimarron Deli in Columbia Falls packs skier lunches. Equipment is available in Whitefish at Outback Ski Shack. Certified ski guides can be hired through Glacier Park Ski Tours.
Phone numbers:	North Fork Hostel, Cabins and Square Peg Ranch (406) 888–5241. Cimarron Deli (406) 892–1490. Glacier National Park (406) 888–7800. Glacier Park Ski Tours (800) 646–6043 ext. 3724. Outback Ski Shack (406) 862–9498. Emergency 911. Cell phones work intermittently in the mountains. Avalanche information (800) 526–5329.

The tiny community of Polebridge is situated just outside the western boundary of Glacier National Park and is 22 miles on rough road from the Canadian border. The gravel road into Polebridge leads to spectacular skiing and snowshoeing in a land of wolves, bears, elk, and other wildlife. The backcountry touring in the Polebridge area includes winter trails into Glacier National Park and nearby on U.S. Forest Service land. Winter visitors enjoy spectacular vistas of the "Crown of the Continent,"

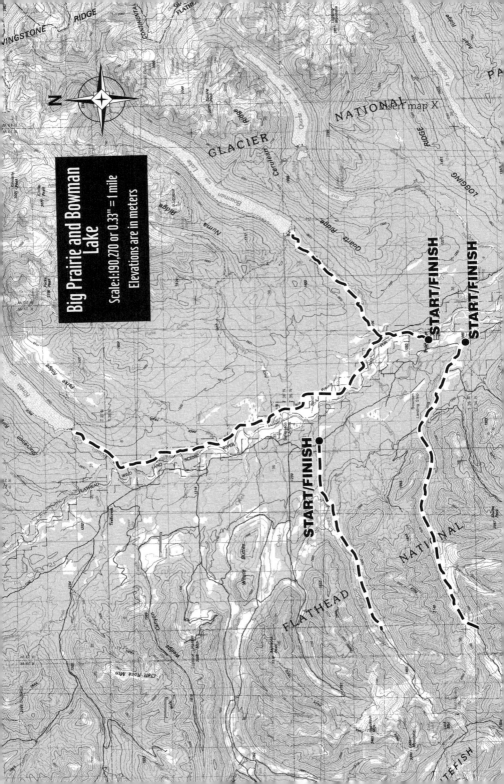

Insert map X

Big Prairie and Bowman Lake

Scale:1:190,270 or 0.33" = 1mile

Elevations are in meters

START/FINISH

START/FINISH

START/FINISH

the nickname for the northern Rockies in Glacier. Polebridge began as a homestead in the remote and wild area of the North Fork of the Flathead River. In 1914, homesteader, packer, and innkeeper Adair Ridge built the Polebridge Mercantile, which remains the centerpiece of the town. The road through town heads north and across the North Fork, a federally designated wild and scenic river, and into Glacier National Park. The town and the Polebridge Ranger Station are named for a bridge over the river made of poles and built nearly a century ago.

Beginners find the trail from Polebridge to Big Prairie an easy introduction to backcountry touring. Rewards include views of the peaks and the river. Although it is possible to begin from town, most people drive 1.3 miles north from town, cross the bridge, and park at the Polebridge Ranger Station. Here the road is both gated and unplowed. The out-and-back trip is from the ranger station is 6 miles over the unplowed road through open meadows.

From the ranger station, the road heads east but almost immediately turns north. The Inside North Fork Road, also called Route 7, intersects here from the south, but skiers should continue north. At .3 mile, the Bowman Creek Campground is visible, then the road to Bowman Lake. Continue heading north. The sign, if not buried in snow, indicates the route to Kintla Lake. Continue north, following the river through open meadow with forest on the right/east. Note that the forest is recovering after the Red Bench Fire of 1988 burned through here. At 3 miles, Big Prairie becomes obvious as a large, natural meadow. Both along the route and at Big Prairie, notice the park's peaks to the east, including the triangular 9,891-foot Rainbow Peak, which rises from Bowman Lake. The Livingston Range to the east and the Whitefish Range to the west provide other scenic backdrops. The road continues to Kintla Lake, a more challenging and much longer route that adds an additional 16 miles to the round trip.

Another, more challenging trail also begins at the ranger station. Just after crossing the bridge over Bowman Creek, the road to Bowman Lake takes off on the right/east. This 12-mile round trip is a challenging day or overnight trip. The trail is on the unplowed road and very obvious, but it can get icy on the hills. Elevation gain is 400 feet on this more difficult route. At approximately mile 4, the trail crests a ridge and becomes less difficult. The marsh on the left/north indicates that the lake is just .2 mile farther. Once at Bowman Lake, watch for deer and other wildlife. The lake's ice is considered unstable. Rangers advise visitors to stay off the lake and away from the lake's outlet. Camping is allowed at Bowman Lake but check with park headquarters for permits. There is no running water or other facilities in winter.

Directions at a glance

From Polebridge Mercantile, ski or drive north on what locals call "River Road" for 1.3 miles. Cross the river on the bridge heading east and pass the Polebridge Ranger Station. The winter trail begins east and immediately turns north.

How to get there

From Columbia Falls, drive north through town on Nucleus Avenue. The road comes to a T intersection at Railroad Street. Turn right/east and stay on this road. It curves north and becomes the North Fork Road #486. Drive the North Fork Road for 35 miles to the marked junction into Polebridge and Glacier National Park. Turn right/east for .2 mile to the Polebridge Mercantile. The North Fork Road is gravel road with a few sections of pavement. It's best to drive during daylight hours. Call the North Fork Hostel, Polebridge Mercantile, or Glacier Park for road conditions if you have any doubt about winter travel.

Avalanche Lake/Going to the Sun Road

Glacier National Park, Montana

Type of trail:	▰▰▰▶ ⬭⬭⬭
Also used by:	Moose
Distance:	13 miles/20.8 kilometers
Terrain:	Gradual climb on Going to the Sun Road, then skier-tracked narrow mountain trail to Avalanche Lake
Trail difficulty:	Easy to advanced
Surface quality:	Skier-tracked
Elevation:	3,280 to 3,905 feet
Food and facilities:	Most facilities in West Glacier close for the winter. The Paola Creek Bed and Breakfast, 18 miles east of West Glacier, hosts guests year round. Ask about trails out the back door in the Great Bear Wilderness. In Coram, the Spruce Park Cafe, a popular hangout, serves good, inexpensive meals. Columbia Falls, Whitefish, and Kalispell have all services. The Cimarron Deli in Columbia Falls packs skier lunches. Equipment is available in Whitefish at Outback Ski Shack, which also rents pulks (ski sleds) in which parents can haul their youngest family members on the trails. Note that a park entrance fee is charged at the West Glacier entrance station. The Apgar Visitor Center is open winter weekends. Certified ski guides are available through Glacier Park Ski Tours. There is a pay phone in the Avalanche Campground that usually works. There's no running water. An outhouse is available at the trailhead and at Avalanche Campground, although snow must be shoveled away from the door.
Phone numbers:	Paola Creek Bed and Breakfast (888) 311–5061 or (406) 888-5061. Spruce Park Cafe (406) 387–5614. Cimarron Deli (406) 892–1490. Glacier National Park (406) 888–7800. Emergency 911. Cell phones work intermittently in the mountains. Avalanche information (800) 526–5329. Glacier Park Ski Tours (800) 646–6043 ext. 3724.

Romantic legend has it that Going to the Sun Mountain, and later the road, is named for a mystic Indian who ascended the 9,642-foot peak to join the sun in eternity. The road, 52 miles long, closes in the fall and reopens usually in June.

From the parking area, the gentle 4-mile route to the Avalanche Campground offers easy skiing and good views of McDonald Creek. The

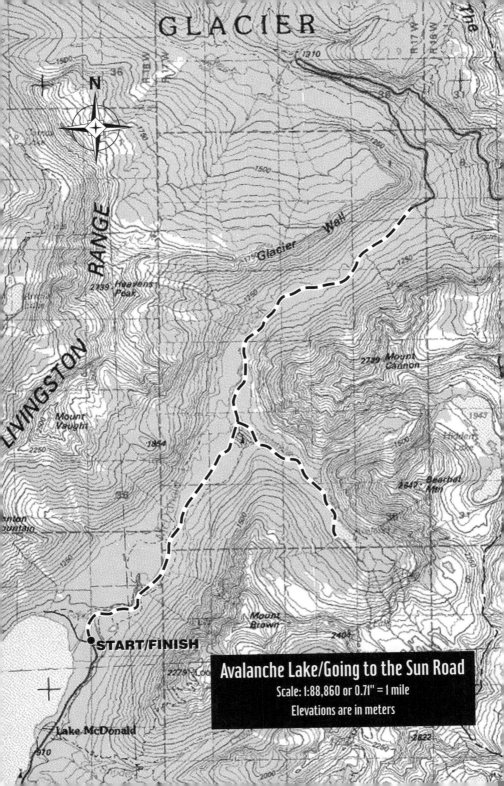

GLACIER

N

GLACIER

Glacier Wall

LIVINGSTON RANGE

Heavens Peak 2739

Mount Vaught

Mount Cannon 2739

Mount Brown 2404

Bearhat Mtn 2847

START/FINISH

Lake McDonald

Avalanche Lake/Going to the Sun Road
Scale: 1:88,860 or 0.71" = 1 mile
Elevations are in meters

forest of cedar and hemlock is surrounded by 8,000-foot mountains. Along the way are several photography opportunities of mountains and McDonald Creek. Sacred Dancing Cascade is on the creek, 1 mile into the trail. Note that moose frequent the Going to the Sun trail in winter. The best advice is to keep a good distance between skier and moose and never approach these unpredictable animals.

The 8-mile round trip visit to Avalanche Picnic Area and campground is a good destination for a day trip. Going to the Sun Road continues, but there is a large and dangerous avalanche path that crosses the road. The road continues to the 6,664-foot elevation at Logan Pass, but skiers should not go beyond the next 4 miles on the road due to extreme avalanche hazards from steep cliffs above and below the road. Eighty-foot snowdrifts often accumulate near the summit and pose extreme danger well into spring. Save those tracks for summer skiing when the road is open!

From the Avalanche Campground, the trail into Avalanche Lake, 2.5 miles/4 kilometers, climbs from 3,406 feet/1,048 meters to 3,884 feet/1,195 meters. The trail begins to the right/east of Going to the Sun Road, just after the vehicle turnoff into the campground and just before the bridge over Avalanche Creek. The trail parallels the creek for .25 mile through a deep forest of western red cedar and western hemlock to the trailhead for Avalanche Lake. The climb to the lake remains in trees;

however, some vantage points near the lake provide a view of Mt. Cannon at 8,952 feet/2,728 meters. Lucky travelers may catch a glimpse of mountain goats. Winter campers need a free backcountry permit to camp at Avalanche Lake.

Snowshoers might consider the 2-mile loop that begins on Going to the Sun Road. One mile into the trail is the Sacred Dancing Cascade on McDonald Creek. Cross on the bridge, turn left/south at the junction across the creek, and head downstream on the west bank of the creek. There is a faint trail, but picking your own route through the trees and along the river is easy. This trail can become slick, and in icy conditions it's better for snowshoeing than skiing. The trail meets the North Lake McDonald Road, where snowshoers turn left/east for a few hundred yards back to the parking area.

The other snowshoe option, the Apgar Nature Trail, begins at the Apgar Visitor Center at the Apgar Campground. The 2.5-mile loop follows a summer trail and offers views of Lake McDonald and surrounding peaks and Lower McDonald Creek. The trail heads west from the visitor center through a mixed conifer forest, then crosses the Camas Road to the confluence of Lower McDonald Creek and the Flathead River. The return trip ends at the visitor center on flat, very easy terrain.

How to get there

West Glacier is 18 miles north of Columbia Falls on U.S. Highway 2. At the West Glacier junction, turn left/north and drive under the railroad trestle through West Glacier. The West Entrance Station is just past the Park Headquarters sign. Drive 2 miles to the T and turn right/east on Going to the Sun Road. Drive 8 miles to the trailhead.

Directions at a glance

Going to the Sun Road is gated at the head of Lake McDonald. Park in the plowed parking area, making sure not to block the gate or the road. There is an outhouse here. The trail begins behind the locked gate heading north, and is a gradual climb on the road for 4 miles to Avalanche Campground.

Autumn Creek

Glacier National Park, Montana

Type of trail:	
Also used by:	Hikers
Distance:	6 miles/9.6 kilometers
Terrain:	Flat in the beginning, then challenging creek crossings and challenging downhill through trees
Trail difficulty:	Easy to more difficult
Surface quality:	Skier-tracked
Elevation:	4,600 to 5,200 feet
Food and facilities:	The closest facility is the Izaak Walton Inn, 17 miles west on U.S. Highway 2, with dining, lodging, equipment rentals, and an Amtrak stop. A few bars may be open near the pass, although hours and days are not dependable. East Glacier, 27 miles east, has few services open in winter. Paola Creek Bed & Breakfast is 18 miles east of West Glacier. Spruce Park Cafe in Coram serves good and inexpensive meals. Closest gas stations are in Coram, on the west side of Marias Pass, and in Browning to the east. Lodging and full services are available 67 miles west in Columbia Falls, 77 miles west in Whitefish, or 80 miles southwest in Kalispell. The Cimarron Deli in Columbia Falls packs skier lunches. Certified ski guides are available through Glacier Park Ski Tours. There are no restroom facilities or running water at either the trailhead or the trail's end. Note that winter camping is permitted in Glacier but that a free backcountry permit is required. Call the park headquarters for details.
Phone numbers:	Glacier National Park (406) 888–7800. Izaak Walton Inn (406) 888–5700. Spruce Park Cafe (406) 387–5614. Cimarron Deli (406) 892–1490. Paola Creek B&B (888) 311–5061. Call (800) 956–6537 for general lodging information. Glacier Park Ski Tours (800) 646–6043 ext. 3724. Emergency 911. Avalanche information (800) 526–5329. Cell phones work intermittently in the mountains.

The trail begins at the historic Marias Pass, the route through the mountains for which the Lewis and Clark Expedition searched unsuccessfully. The 5,200-foot pass is one of the lowest routes over the Continental Divide. While the pass was used by the Salish and Kootenai Indians trekking to buffalo hunts on the plains, the warrior Blackfeet Indians kept most early explorers away. It wasn't until the late 1880s that

a Great Northern Railway surveyor found the pass. The railroad punched a route through in 1891. The highway was completed in 1930.

As skiers get their gear ready, and before crossing the railroad tracks, the view above the trees to the northwest is worth a photo. Little Dog Mountain, at 8,610 feet/2,624.5 meters is probably named for Piegan Indian Chief Little Dog, or Imiti-koan, meaning puppy. The trail travels toward Little Dog Mountain in a lodgepole forest near the Continental Divide.

Once in the trees, the trail is a gentle single track. Three Bear Lake at .66 mile is a good turn-around point for beginners; the trail becomes more challenging after this point. The lake itself was a railroad water reservoir a century ago.

Directions at a glance

- Leave a shuttle vehicle parked on the west side of the pass in a small, plowed parking area on U.S. Highway 2 at mile marker 193.8.
- Drive to the Marias Pass Summit and park either at the Marias Pass Steven's Monument (a miniature of the Washington Monument) or on the north side of U.S. 2 between the highway and the railroad tracks.
- Carry skis northwest across the tracks. Use caution when walking over the busy railroad lines.
- Ski 40 yards to the park border and the marked trailhead.
- At 1 mile, the trail splits east and west. Take the left/west turn and follow the route 5 miles to shuttle vehicle.

At 1 mile from the trailhead, the trail splits. Turn left at this junction. The trail continues in trees between the seldom-visible Blacktail Hills to the south and Little Dog and Elk Mountain to the north. Look for the orange trail markers on trees. There will be a few challenging creek crossings where skiers will need to side-step down and up steep banks.

The Autumn Creek Trail suddenly breaks out of the trees into a scenic, high-mountain cirque. This area can be extremely windy and if weather brings snow, white-out conditions can occur.

While the slopes on the cirque are quite tempting for telemarkers, avalanche danger is extreme. Most skiers choose the meadow area for a picnic, far from the avalanche chutes. The trail crosses several avalanche paths, but the crossings are low and over run-out zones. Here the route is sometimes difficult to find on the open slope. Look for orange markers on the trees to the southwest and the obvious drainage of Autumn Creek.

The last 2 miles down to the highway descends through trees and can get icy and covered with slippery pine needles. The trail follows the right/west side of Autumn Creek to the highway. The final slope down to the highway ends on a jeep road with a locked gate.

How to get there

From Kalispell and Glacier International Airport, take U.S. 2 east through Columbia Falls and past West Glacier. Follow signs for East Glacier. Marias Pass is 77 miles from Glacier International Airport.

Essex Trail Complex/Izaak Walton Inn

East Glacier, Montana

Type of trail:

Also used by: Telemarkers; grooming machines may be on trails.

Distance: 19.2 miles/32 kilometers

Terrain: Gently rolling to steeper hills; includes telemark practice bowl

Trail difficulty: Novice to intermediate; a few advanced routes

Surface quality: Groomed for classic, skate, and snowshoe

Elevation: 3,000 to 5,000 feet

Food and facilities: The Izaak Walton Inn, with full-service dining, lodging, ski and snowshoe rentals, and gift shop, is located at the trailhead. The restaurant serves wholesome meals, including homemade bread, soups, and pies, and is open for breakfast, lunch, and dinner. The Izaak Walton Inn offers unique lodging in the refurbished 1939 lodge and in four renovated Great Northern Railway cabooses. Cabooses are fully insulated and heated with cooking and bath facilities. The lodge originally housed Great Northern Railway train crews. The inn has rental equipment, including pulks for parents to bring along their youngest children. The inn is just across the highway from Glacier National Park, where guests can ski with or without a guide.

Phone numbers: USFS District Ranger, Hungry Horse (406) 387–5243. Izaak Walton Inn (406) 888–5700; www.izaakwaltoninn.com. Emergency 911. Cell phones work intermittently in the mountains. Avalanche advisory (406) 257–8402 or in Montana (800) 526–5329.

The Essex Ski Trail system is a combination of roads and trails over gentle grades and open slopes. Different vantage points offer views into both Glacier National Park and the Great Bear Wilderness. Because the trails are due west of the Continental Divide, early winter storms leave enough snow to open the tracks by the first of December and often before Thanksgiving through the spring. Izaak Walton Inn's annual "Snow Rodeo" and "Kick Out the Kinks" fun events and ski races are traditionally the first weekend in December. The inn offers ski and snowshoe guided trips into Glacier National Park. The inn and the nearby creek and mountain were named for English author and fisherman Izaak Walton, who wrote *The Compleat Angler* over three centuries ago.

N

BM
3818

Essex ▲

Creek

BOUNDARY

Essex PO

Dickey

3800

FORK

3820

TRACK

3833

11

FLATHEAD

3800

4600

5000

4200

Essex

BM
3860

4130

WT

4200

**START//
FINISH**

3800

1b

5000

14

Creek

GREAT

Campground

Walton
Ranger Station

4000

NATIONAL

4000

4000

6338

RIVER

NORTHERN

3913

Tank

FORK

23

Creek

Essex Trail Complex/Izaak Walton Inn
Scale: 1:24,550 or 2.58" = 1 mile

Skiers must carry skis and use caution when climbing the steel foot-bridge over the railroad tracks to the trailhead. Trails begin with a short uphill heading north before relaxing into rolling terrain. A favorite evening jaunt is the lit Starlight Trail, a 1-kilometer loop open until 11 P.M. "so guests can work off that last piece of cobbler," says innkeeper Larry Vielleux. From the trailhead, the Starlight Trail goes northwest and makes a counterclockwise loop that passes both Telemark Hill and the four cabooses. At each junction, skiers stay to the left for this 1 kilometer loop.

Kids love the 2.9-kilometer Pileated Trail of Lower Essex Loop, which features interpretive signs along the way. The signs give youngsters a chance to identify animal tracks and are a good excuse to take a breather along this intermediate route. Skiers follow directions to Starlight Trail, then at the second junction follow the signs turning right/west to Pileated. Pileated Trail hooks up to Starlight at Junction Circle. Just as Pileated begins its loop back south and then east, skiers can opt for another 1.6 kilometers on the more advanced Towering Pines loop. Like its namesake, this trail makes dwarfs of skiers among the giant timbers as they climb to Kendi's crossing over Essex Creek. There's a rustic chair swing overlooking the creek.

From Junction Circle, several trail options direct skiers to the 3-kilometer Essex Creek Trail and beyond to the 1.5-kilometer Highline Loop.

Swinging benches on the top of the Essex Trail on the Highline and the Towering Pines trails provide opportunities to take in the view during the tour. This route includes descending the curves of Awesome Hill.

The Middle Fork River Trail's gentle beginner terrain provides views of the Middle Fork of the Flathead River and beyond into Glacier National Park. For this 5.2-kilometer loop, skiers start at the trailhead and turn right/north at the first junction onto Essex Road. After 2 kilometers, Essex Road meets Dickey Creek Road, where skiers turn right/northeast and meet the railroad tracks. Remove skis and use extreme caution when crossing the railroad tracks and later the highway. Once across the highway, the Middle Fork River Trail heads east toward the river, then back toward the highway near the Izaak Walton Inn. Note that the trail crosses some private land and visitors are asked to respect the hosts' privacy. The trail can be skied in either direction.

The recommended warm-up route for snowshoers is the Wylder Loop, a 1.5-kilometer route that offers great photo opportunities of the Izaak Walton Inn. From the trailhead, snowshoers take the first right/north turn onto Wylder. For a longer jaunt, snowshoers follow the Starlight Trail to the third junction, which is the snowed-in Essex Road, and turn left/west. Snowshoers (and skiers) on this out-and-back, 3.5-kilometer trail should turn back at Horse-Camp Cutoff, beyond which avalanche danger exists.

How to get there

From Kalispell and Glacier International Airport, take U.S. 2 east past West Glacier and follow the signs to East Glacier. The inn is 60 miles from Kalispell at mile marker 180. Many guests ride Amtrak to the door of the Izaak Walton Inn.

Ole Creek

Glacier National Park, Montana

Type of trail:	━━━ 🐾
Also used by:	Telemarkers, alpine touring skiers, wildlife
Distance:	10 miles/16 kilometers
Terrain:	Hilly and mountainous
Trail difficulty:	Moderate to expert
Surface quality:	Snowshoe-packed
Elevation:	3,900 to 4,800 feet
Food and facilities:	Closest facility is the Izaak Walton Inn, .9 mile west of Ole Creek and the Walton Ranger Station on U.S. Highway 2. The inn offers dining, lodging, equipment rentals, and an Amtrak stop. A few bars may be open near the pass, although hours and days are not dependable. East Glacier, 35 miles east, has few services open in winter. Spruce Park Cafe in Coram serves good and inexpensive meals. The closest gas station is in Coram to the west and Browning to the east. Lodging and full services are available in Columbia Falls, Whitefish, and Kalispell. The Cimarron Deli in Columbia Falls packs skier lunches. Certified ski guides are available through Glacier Park Ski Tours. There are no restroom facilities or running water at the trailheads. Winter camping is permitted in Glacier National Park but a free backcountry permit is required. Call park headquarters for details.
Phone numbers:	Glacier National Park (406) 888–7800. Izaak Walton Inn (406) 888–5700. Emergency 911. Avalanche information (800) 526–5329. Cell phones work intermittently in the mountains. Spruce Park Cafe (406) 387–5614. Cimarron Deli (406) 892–1490. Call (800) 956–6537 for general lodging information. Glacier Park Ski Tours (800) 646–6043 ext. 3724.

The area between Fielding and Ole Creek, near the top of the Continental Divide, receives several hundred inches of snow every winter and often has snow early and late season. Fielding, named for the Fielding Siding where trains can pass each other, was once next to a rough-and-tumble town called McCarthysville. When the Great Northern Railway laid tracks here in 1891, a Chinese kitchen stood at Fielding in between sets of tracks. Although the town existed only three winters, tales abound of its toughness. Body counts during spring thaw revealed min-

Ole Creek, Glacier National Park
Scale: 1:100,570 or .63" = 1 mile
Elevations are in meters

START

FINISH

N

Insert map

ers, boom town characters, Chinese workers, and outlaws who lived and died there. Ole Creek, named for a Scandinavian trapper, was called Buckskin Horse Creek by the Kootenai Indians.

Skiers and snowshoers who choose to do the entire 10-mile route from Fielding Picnic Area to Ole Creek and down to the Walton Ranger Station should plan for a very long day or else come equipped for winter camping along the trail. Check with the Park Service before you make an overnight stay, both to obtain a backcountry permit and for information regarding snow bridges crossing Ole Creek. Adventurers who wish for an easier day trip can travel either from Fielding to Ole Creek and back out for a 7-mile round trip, or from Walton Ranger Station to Ole Creek, a 2.2-mile round trip.

From Fielding Picnic Area, travel north by northwest .9 mile to the

railroad tracks. Remove skis and watch for trains while crossing. The track area can be very slippery so use caution. The trail passes the closed Fielding Patrol Cabin. The trail climbs from 4,500 to 4,800 feet, where it crosses a small creek coming off Elk Mountain. Elk Mountain rises on the east side of the trail at 7,835 feet. Continue for 1.75 miles following the orange trail markers to the intersection with Ole Creek. This is a good turn-around point because there is no bridge here. If you're continuing down Ole Creek to Walton Ranger Station, cross the creek here using extreme caution on snow bridges. Numerous avalanche paths dump into the Ole Creek drainage. A wintering herd of elk live along Ole Creek. The route descends to 3,900 feet at Walton. The final 1.1 miles crosses Ole Creek on a suspended foot bridge.

Directions at a glance

From the Fielding Picnic Area parking lot at the "chain-up" area, ski north by northwest on the wide jeep trail/ski trail. From Walton Ranger Station, ski west behind the log buildings, past the summer-only backcountry parking area and past the pit toilet. The trailhead is well marked.

The relatively easy snowshoe or ski from Walton Ranger Station up to the footbridge crossing Ole Creek is a popular route through conifer forest to the confluence of Ole Creek and the Middle Fork of the Flathead River. From the ranger station, travel east through the picnic area and past the backcountry parking area. The trailhead is next to the closed pit toilet. The trail climbs about 100 feet over 1.1 miles; however, since the trail does get quite a bit of snowshoe traffic, the trail can be narrow and deep. Skiers may want climbing skins for the uphill or choose to climb on the side of the trail. Just before the footbridge, a horse-packing sign points left/west. This short trail leads to the confluence of the creek and river, providing views of the surrounding mountains. The footbridge presents an interesting sensation for skiing or snowshoeing.

From the bridge, the trail climbs above the creek and follows it east. At 1 mile, the trail meets the Boundary Trail, where telemarkers and alpine touring skiers with climbing skins venture off for extreme turns on the 6,919-foot Scalplock Mountain.

How to get there

From Essex, the Fielding trailhead is 13 miles east at the "chain-up" area on Highway 2 at mile marker 192, just west of the Fielding Picnic Area. From Essex, the Walton Ranger Station and Ole Creek trailhead are .9 mile east, just across the Highway 2 bridge. Park next to the log ranger buildings.

Glacier Nordic Center
Whitefish, Montana

Type of trail:	▬▬ ◄
Also used by:	The Center is for Nordic skiers only.
Distance:	7.2 miles/12 kilometers
Terrain:	Shorter loops are flat. Longer loops offer a variety of hills and flats.
Trail difficulty:	Easy beginner loops and intermediate terrain
Surface quality:	Groomed skate lane and classic track (groomed daily)
Elevation:	3,080 to 3,160 feet
Food and facilities:	Trail-side restaurants include the full-service Grouse Mountain Lodge and the dinner-only Whitefish Lake Restaurant. There is an outhouse at the trailhead. Ski rentals, lessons, and snacks are available from the Outback Ski Shack at the trailhead. Whitefish offers several grocery stores, convenience stores, gas stations, restaurants, and lodging facilities. Guests at The Garden Wall Bed & Breakfast find luxury lodging, a gourmet breakfast, and tips on skiing in the region from the hosts, who are dedicated cross-country skiers. The Buffalo Cafe serves hearty skier breakfasts. The Whitefish Times coffee house is a good place to warm up with lattes. Lodging and restaurants available at The Big Mountain Ski and Summer Resort, 8 miles north of Whitefish.
Phone numbers:	Glacier Nordic Ski School (406) 862–9498. Outback Ski Shack (406) 862–9498, winter only. For trail conditions call Glacier Nordic Club Snow Phone at (406) 881–4230, winter only. The Garden Wall Bed & Breakfast (888) 530–1700. The Big Mountain Nordic Center at the Outpost Ski Shop (406) 862–2946, winter only. Central Reservations/The Big Mountain (800) 858–5439 or (406) 862–1900. For general travel information, contact the Whitefish Chamber of Commerce (877) 862–3548. Emergency: 911. Mountains interfere with some cell phones.

Beginners have great luck on the well-groomed trails here, which are right in town and close to hot chocolate. Ski lessons are available daily from certified instructors at the Glacier Nordic Ski School, through the Outback Ski Shack (reservations requested). The grooming and the scenic terrain draw ski racers to these trails on the Whitefish Lake Golf Course.

START/
FINISH

Whitefish

Glacier Nordic Center
Scale: 1:19,200 or 3.30" = 1 mile

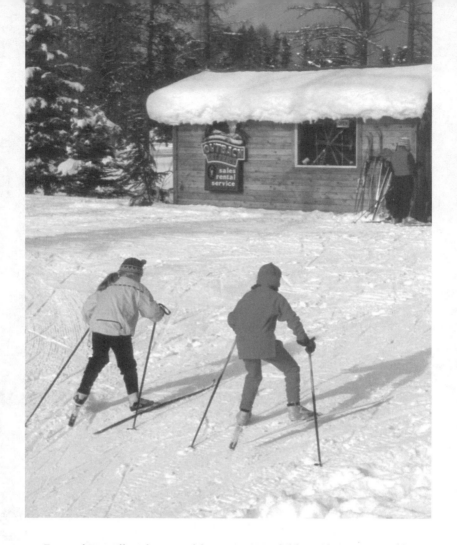

From the trailhead, several loops are available and run in one direction. Signs here provide directions. Directly behind the Outback Ski Shack is the beginner .5-kilometer Cookie Loop. It's wide, it's flat, and there's even an old school bell hidden in the trees for the kids to ring. The Cookie Loop travels clockwise, beginning west for .2 kilometer, turns right/north at the first junction, continues 30 feet, and then turns right/east again at another junction to return to the trailhead. From this second junction, the school bell is hidden in the trees on the left/north. Look for kids or their tracks heading off into the woods about 50 meters after the junction. The bell hangs in the trees off the trail. After ringing the bell and returning to the trail, the route briefly splits; continue east through a row of chubby evergreens and back to the trailhead, or turn left and go over a small hill before returning to the trailhead.

Directions at a glance

Trails begin from the parking lot of the Whitefish Lake Golf Club at the Whitefish Lake Restaurant and immediately in front of the Outback Ski Shack on the west side of the parking area. Lakeside trails lead west behind the Outback Ski Shack. Grouse Mountain side trails head south through a tunnel under the highway.

The 4.2-kilometer Lake Loop takes off from the Cookie Loop at the first intersection, runs up and down a short hill, and then leisurely winds through trees and down to a point overlooking Whitefish Lake. A shortcut back to the Cookie Loop makes for a 2.9-kilometer ski that connects at the second junction of the Cookie Loop just before the school bell.

Trails on the south side of the highway are accessed through the skier tunnel known as Grattan's Shaft. Use caution in this tunnel: It may be icy, and sometimes gravel from the highway above is washed onto the snow. Some skiers walk rather than ski through the tunnel. The trails on the south side run counterclockwise and begin with a schuss south past the steps of Grouse Mountain Lodge. A .5-kilometer loop cuts back to the trailhead 75 meters past the south end of the lodge. The Tinkerbell, Lost Coon, MacKenzie's Dogleg, and Karrow Loops are accessed by continuing south on the Grouse Mountain Loop.

A very quiet and more challenging loop is the 3.5-kilometer Lost Coon Loop. Continue south on the Grouse Loop and follow the groomed trail around Tinkerbell Loop; Lost Coon's access begins just south of a rock-walled pond and a service shed. Skiers should remove skis to cross the paved Fairway Drive. The trail passes along Lost Coon Lake, loops back near a horse barn, along the lake again, and through a grove of aspen trees. Skiers walk back across Fairway Drive to the Grouse Mountain trails for a round trip of 7.5 kilometers, including all the Grouse-side loops.

A very attractive aspect of skiing on these tracks is the string of lights for night skiing. Tinkerbell's 2.8 kilometers of trails stay lit until 11:00 P.M. every night.

How to get there

Glacier Nordic Center is 1 mile west of downtown Whitefish on Highway 93 North. Turn right/north just after the Whitefish Cemetery and park in the Whitefish Lake Golf Course and Restaurant parking lot.

The Big Mountain Nordic Trails
Whitefish, Montana

Type of trail:	▬▬ ◉ ◀
Also used by:	Walkers
Distance:	9.6 miles/16 kilometers plus 2.5-mile hill climb
Terrain:	Hilly
Trail difficulty:	Moderate to difficult
Surface quality:	Machine-groomed daily
Elevation:	4,500 to 7,000 feet
Food and facilities:	Ski rentals are available at the Outpost Lodge at the trailhead and in Whitefish at Outback Ski Shack. Several lodging facilities are available on The Big Mountain, including Kandahar Lodge and Hibernation House. More lodging and all services are available in nearby Whitefish, such as The Garden Wall Bed & Breakfast and Hidden Moose Lodge. Excellent on-mountain restaurants include Hellroaring Saloon and Eatery and Cafe Kandahar. The photographers in Mountain Photography and First Tracks Trading Post will make unique photographs of skiers using the Glacier Park peaks as backdrop.
Phone numbers:	The Big Mountain Nordic Center at the Outpost Ski Shop (406) 862–2946, winter only. Outback Ski Shack (406) 862–9498. Central Reservations/The Big Mountain (800) 858–5439 or (406) 862–1900. Snowphone (406) 862–7669. Kandahar Lodge (406) 862–6098. The Garden Wall Bed & Breakfast (888) 530–1700. Hidden Moose Lodge (406) 862–6516. Mountain Photography and First Tracks Trading Post (406) 862–6905. Whitefish Chamber of Commerce (877) 862–3548. Emergency 911. Mountains interfere with cell phones. Avalanche advisory (406) 257–8402 or in Montana (800) 526–5329.

The charm of The Big Mountain's Nordic trails include well-groomed, well-marked routes, challenging terrain, hot chocolate and chow at the trailhead, and a fun innertubing hill nearby. There are also ten ski lifts and excellent telemarking terrain. Although Big Mountain is primarily an alpine ski resort offering over 3,500 skiable acres, cross-country skiers, snowshoers, and backcountry skiers put in mileage on the tracks and on the mountain. Snowshoers not only follow the cross-country ski route but enjoy climbing to the top of the 7,000-foot peak. Alpine touring skiers also frequently climb the mountain, using climbing skins for the

The Big Mountain Nordic Trails

Scale: 1:12,310 or 5.15" = 1 mile

N

START/FINISH

Pond

Ski Resort

SKI LIFT

FLATHEAD

NATIONAL FOREST

4600

4400

4845

4652

4578

ascent. The view from the summit includes the peaks of Glacier National Park to the east, the Canadian Rockies to the north, the Salish and Cabinet Mountains in the west, and the Swan Range and Whitefish and Flathead Lakes to the south. First-time cross-country skiers should consider skiing on Whitefish's Glacier Nordic Trails instead of The Big Mountain Nordic Trails; however, early- and late-season snow coverage is much better on the mountain.

Before stepping into bindings, skiers and snowshoers should stop by the Outpost for a trail pass and to ask about trail conditions. The cross-country trails are groomed with one classic and one skate lane and generally make clockwise loops. Snowshoers are asked stay off the classic tracks. From the Outpost, the intermediate Gopher Trail, a 5.5-kilometer loop, is a popular ski that offers glimpses of the Flathead Valley below and the ski runs above. Gopher climbs through timber along a wide trail. Big downhills are well marked but skiers should look ahead for one sharp turn at the bottom of the first downhill. A challenging loop, the 1.5-kilometer Badger Trail, takes off from and returns to Gopher shortly after the first long downhill.

A short loop near the trailhead, the 1.5-kilometer Weasel Trail, begins with the short downhill at the trailhead. Ski south and loop back along the well-marked trail. Skiers can continue onto the advanced terrain of the Wolverine Trail, which takes off from Weasel on the western edge of the pond. From Wolverine, skiers can dip down to other ponds on the Cedar Loop, a 2.5-kilometer trail, and finish on Pine Marten Loop to the Outpost.

Hill climbing has become very popular aboard snowshoes or on telemark or alpine touring skis fitted with climbing skins. Several routes to the summit provide outstanding views after the 2,500-foot, 2.5-mile climb. The ski school offers guided snowshoeing and suggests using ski poles for balance. An alpine ski map is available at the Outpost. From the Outpost begin heading east on Inspiration Ski Trail, which parallels the first kilometer of the Gopher Trail. The best choice is to climb along the right edge of the ski runs near the trees, keeping in mind that snowboarders may hit jumps going into or out of the trees. At the first intersection, continue right/east on the jeep road, which is called Expressway Run. After passing six intersecting ski runs coming onto Expressway, the trail meets Russell Street. Stay to the right on Russell Street, which will climb northeast and along the ski area boundary. Near the top, the trail turns northwest and heads to the Summit. The final slope, where Summit House becomes visible, can be extremely busy with alpine skier traffic so use caution here. Once at the summit, snowshoers can choose to ride the chairlift down the mountain for free.

How to get there

Glacier International Airport is twenty minutes from Whitefish. Amtrak stops in Whitefish. Shuttle service is available. From Whitefish, drive north on Baker Street. Go over the viaduct and continue north on Baker, which becomes Wisconsin and then East Lake Shore. Drive 3 miles to Big Mountain Road, turn right/north, and drive up 5 miles. At the sign for the Outpost, turn right/east and follow the road .5 mile down to the Outpost. Look for parking at any of several parking areas but do not park at the Outpost turn-around.

Directions at a glance

From the Outpost Lodge, trails begin east of the building at the parking lot level. For the easier trails, begin by skiing down the short, steep slope to Weasel Loop. More challenging trails take off from Weasel or skiers climb the first hill heading north to Gopher.

Round Meadows
Whitefish, Montana

Type of trail:	▬▬ 🍩 ◁
Also used by:	Mule deer and occasional moose
Distance:	9 miles/14.4 kilometers
Terrain:	Meadows and forested rolling hills
Trail difficulty:	Easiest to moderately difficult
Surface quality:	Machine-groomed weekly and skier-tracked
Elevation:	3,200 to 3,400 feet
Food and facilities:	An outhouse is open at the trailhead. Free trail maps are in a mailbox at the trailhead. Whitefish, 13 miles southeast, has restaurants, lodging, and visitor information. Ski equipment is available at the Outback Ski Shack. Trail condition information is available at the Tally Lake Ranger Station in Whitefish.
Phone numbers:	Tally Lake Ranger Station (406) 863–5400. Outback Ski Shack (406) 862–9498, winter only. For general travel information, contact the Whitefish Chamber of Commerce (877) 862–3548. The Garden Wall Bed & Breakfast staff skis trails in the region and can offer current trail advice (888) 530–1700. Emergency 911. The mountains may interfere with the use of cellular phones.

Although Round Meadows is only 13 miles from Whitefish, it presents a rural ski experience. It's rare that skiers will encounter other ski parties on this trail system. Trails travel through meadows and evergreen forests and offer views of the Whitefish Mountain Range. Round Meadows is named for the meadow along the Round Meadows Loop. According to the U.S. Forest Service, about 12,000 years ago, when the Continental Ice Sheet retreated, large blocks of ice remained. The blocks' weight created depressions in the ground, which resulted in shallow lakes. Gradually the lakes filled with silt and organic matter, creating the meadows we see today. When snow melts in spring, the meadows fill with melt water and once again resemble lakes. All trail intersections have trail signs.

The trails at Round Meadows depart from the Round Meadows Loop, a 3.3-mile intermediate trail. Much of the trail follows roads or a wide path so skiers can ski side-by-side. Heading north from the parking area, the trail takes a straight course north by northwest for a mile. Skiers will pass the junction for Chechako on the right/west at .75 mile and the end of Chechako loop at 2 miles. Continue around the loop past the Logan Creek junction, where the Round Meadows Loop turns back south. At the junction with Fox Run Trail, the route narrows. Turn left/east and follow the trail back to the parking area.

The 2.68-mile Chechako Loop begins on the Round Meadows Loop. After .75 mile, and at the first intersection, turn right/east and ski the intermediate Chechako Loop. About a half mile of Chechako is narrow, but most the trail is fairly wide. Chechako provides views of the Whitefish Mountain Range and the surrounding forests.

The Logan Creek Loop, considered most difficult, is a 1.1-mile route that is accessed from Chechako Loop at 2 miles. From Chechako, turn right/west onto Logan Creek Loop. After a few hundred yards, the trail begins to follow Logan Creek. Skiers are among aspen, birch, cottonwoods, and fir trees. Mule deer and mountain lions frequent the area, as do marten and weasel; it's a good place to find and identify animal tracks. The ice formations along the creek make carrying a camera worthwhile.

Other trails that take off from the Round Meadows Loop include Fox Run Trail, a more difficult .9 mile route, and Lookout, a most difficult .9 mile trail. Note that all of Round Meadows trails are closed to dogs.

How to get there

From Whitefish, drive Highway 93 north for 10.2 miles. Turn left/southwest on Farm-to-Market Road at the sign for Round Meadows. Drive 1.7 miles, then turn right/north onto Star Meadows Road at the Round Meadows sign. Drive 1 mile to the parking area for Round Meadows on the right/north.

Directions at a glance

From the Round Meadows parking area, the trailhead is at the north end of the Round Meadows parking area.

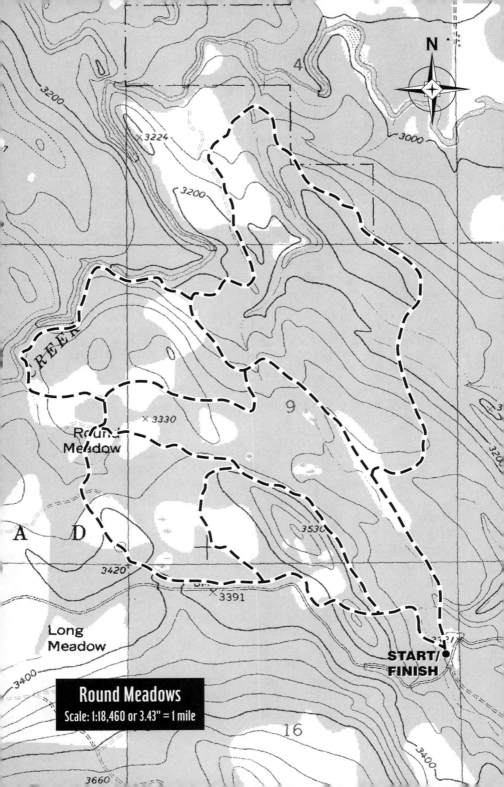

N

× 3224

3200

3200

3000

4

9

× 3330

Round
Meadow

A   D

× 3330

3530

3420

× 3391

3400

3660

Long
Meadow

START/
FINISH

16

Round Meadows
Scale: 1:18,460 or 3.43" = 1 mile

South Flower Creek Trails/Libby Area Trails

Libby, Montana

Type of trail:	▬ ● ◀
Also used by:	Snowmobiles, wildlife
Distance:	9 miles/15 kilometers
Terrain:	Forested rolling hills and gentle terrain
Trail difficulty:	Beginner to advanced
Surface quality:	Machine-groomed twice weekly
Elevation:	2,700 to 3,300 feet
Food and facilities:	There are no facilities at the trailhead, but all services are just ten minutes away in Libby. Snowshoe Ski Haus has equipment rentals. Try the Hidden Chapel restaurant for dinner in an old church. The Venture Inn has good lunch and dinner. Locals go to Henry's or the Libby Cafe for breakfast. Lodging includes the Super 8, the Venture Inn/Best Western, the Kootenai Country Inn, and Serenity Place.
Phone numbers:	Kootenai XC Ski Club (406) 293–2441. Kootenai National Forest (406) 295–4693. Libby Chamber of Commerce (406) 293–4167. Troy Chamber of Commerce (406) 295–4216. Snowshoe Specialty Sport (406) 293–3890. Super 8 (800) 800–8000. The Venture Inn/Best Western (800) 528–1234. Kootenai Country Inn 293–7878. Serenity Place 293–9324.

Mountainous northwest Montana is known for thick timber, remote mountains, large rivers, and few people. Many landmarks are named for the Kootenai Indians. Libby and nearby Troy grew from rough-and-tumble, turn-of-the century towns into hubs for recreation, timber, and mining industries. Skiing began in Libby in the 1930s and '40s on the Skidale Slope, a 200-foot hill equipped with a rope tow and frequented by Scandinavian folks in the area. Alpine skiers now ride the country's longest T-bar at Turner Mountain. Nordic skiers and snowshoers have several backcountry trails in the area, as well as the groomed South Flower Creek Cross-Country Ski Course just ten minutes from Libby. The Kootenai Cross-Country Ski Club maintains the trails on city, state, and federal lands.

The 15-kilometer South Flower Creek trails are groomed twice weekly for classic and skate skiers and snowshoers (on the skate lane only). From the trailhead, skiers begin generally on the easy, 1-kilometer Shorty's Loop heading west from the gated road and skiing counter-

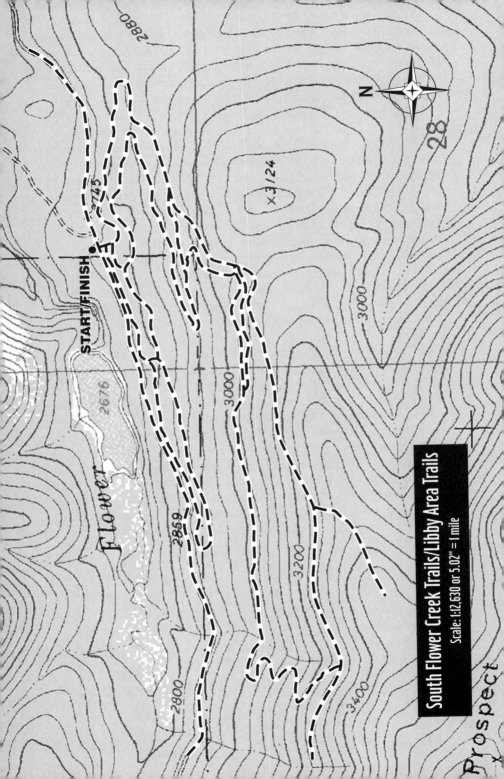

START/FINISH

N

28

Flower

2880

2745

2676

2859

2800

3000

3000

3200

3400

×3124

South Flower Creek Trails/Libby Area Trails
Scale: 1:12,630 or 5.02" = 1 mile

Prospect

The bigger kids love to connect to Roller Coaster from Shorty's, adding 1.5 kilometers and 120 feet of elevation gain to the ski. Roller Coaster was named by the local cross-country ski team kids for the five hills on the return trip. The kids learn to ski fast enough to catch air over the bumps. Rollercoaster cruises through a partially logged area and past a frozen pond on the return trip. All trails are signed at intersections.

A longer ski, the 14-kilometer (round trip) Treasure Tour, Road #4729, begins at the trailhead. Treasure first travels south for .1 kilometer, then turns east. At .6 kilometer, Treasure Tour turns southwest for the remainder of the route to Treasure Mountain. The wide trail gradually climbs past the intersection with Tongue Dragger to Jabber Junction, named by the ski team kids for the spot where they stretch muscles and tongues after a 1.5-kilometer warm-up. From Jabber Junction, stay on the left/southernmost trail to continue on Treasure Tour. Be prepared for thirty to forty-five minutes of climbing; there's a 600-foot elevation gain in 3 kilometers. After the climb, the trail becomes flat and rolling. The grooming ends at the 7-kilometer point. Skiers can continue on 4 kilometers of skier-tracked trail to 3,300 feet at the base of Treasure Mountain, a proposed alpine ski area in the Cabinet Mountains. Note that part of this old road is open to snowmobiles but is used infrequently.

The Forest Service lists several backcountry ski tours in the Libby–Troy area. Most popular is the Rainbow Lake Trail, 22 miles north of Libby and 2 miles north of Turner Mountain Ski Area on Pipe Creek Road. From the trailhead at about 4,400 feet elevation, ski southwest on a Forest Service road that climbs gently for 2.8 kilometers. The trail then becomes steeper and goes through a clearcut. Most skiers turn around here and return on the same trail. You can continue, however, and ski the Summit Trail to the top of Flatiron Mountain. The summit of the 5,891-foot Flatiron in the Purcell Mountain Range is another 9 kilometers. Blue trail markers on trees line the Summit Trail. Telemarkers and snowboarders make turns down open bowls off the summit trail. Ask locally about avalanche conditions. There is a view of Roderick Mountain to the northwest, and of Big Creek Baldy, which has a fire lookout on top, to the southeast.

How to get there

From Libby, drive south on Highway 2 for .5 mile to the BP gas station. Turn right/south on Shaughnessy Road. Go up the hill; at top turn left on Snowshoe Road and drive .25 mile. Turn right/southwest on Granite Lake Road and drive .5 mile, passing the gated road, then turn right on an unmarked road. Look for a small cross-country ski sign and drive through the open gate. Drive 1.1 miles and park in the lot on the left.

Directions at a glance

From the parking area, step across the metal gate and head south and ski up the road 20 feet. Trails begin on the right/west.

Blacktail Mountain
Lakeside, Montana

Type of trail:	▬ ⬤ ◄
Also used by:	Snowmobilers have their own trails nearby.
Distance:	25 miles/40.5 kilometers
Terrain:	Some flats but primarily hilly and mountainous
Trail difficulty:	Some easy terrain leads to more difficult
Surface quality:	Machine-groomed as needed surfaces for single track and packed for skating and snowshoeing
Elevation:	4,170 to 5,500 feet
Food and facilities:	Blacktail Mountain Lodge at the summit sells burgers, beer, hot chocolate, and fries in Muleys. It is open winter only, Wednesday through Sunday, 9 A.M. to 6 P.M. Lodging, restaurants, and other services are open in Lakeside; for example, Bluestone Grill & Tap, for dining, and the Stoner Creek Merchantile deli.. Equipment can be found in Kalispell at Rocky Mountain Outfitters and Sportsman Ski Haus.
Phone numbers:	For trail conditions call Flathead County Parks and Recreation at (406) 758–5800. Call Bigfork Ranger District for a free map (406) 837–7500. There are no phones at the trailheads; the nearest phones are farther up the Blacktail Road at the alpine ski area. Rocky Mountain Outfitters (406) 752–2446. Sportsman Ski Haus (406) 755–6486 Lakeside Chamber of Commerce (405) 844–3715. Emergency 911 works from Lakeside and from the summit at the alpine ski area. There are some exposed slopes that could produce avalanches. Contact the Avalanche Report locally at (406) 257–8402 or (800) 526–5329.

Blacktail's trails offer fantastic views of the surrounding mountains, the Flathead Valley, and Flathead Lake. Often, when the Flathead Valley floor is under fog or clouds, Blacktail visitors ski or snowshoe above the clouds and into sunshine. Four different mountain ranges are visible from parts of the trail system, in addition to views into Lake Mary Ronan and Flathead Lake. Dogs are not allowed on the trails. Watch for the mule deer, also called blacktail deer, that inhabit the area.

The 10-kilometer/6-mile Alpine Loop is the easiest route on Blacktail. It begins and ends at the upper trailhead. Flathead County Parks suggests that trail users ski this route clockwise, leaving the parking lot at the marked trailhead. The final slope back to the parking area drops from

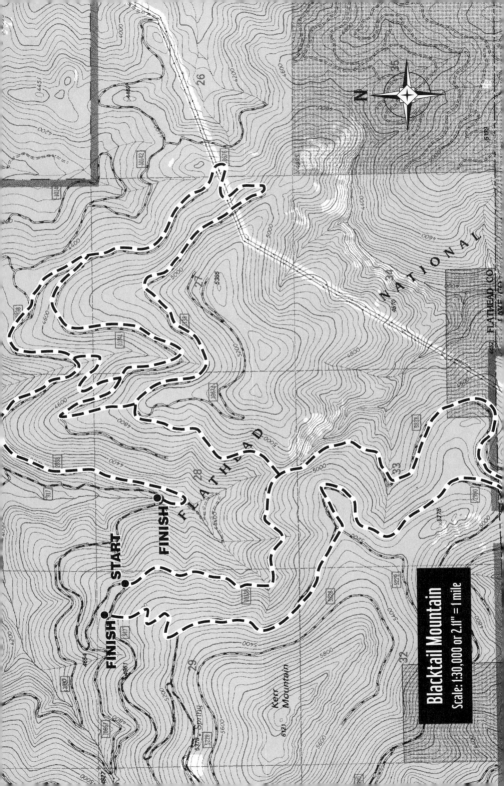

Blacktail Mountain
Scale: 1:30,000 or 2.11" = 1 mile

5,200 feet down to about 4,800 feet on switchbacks.

Some skiers choose to bring two vehicles, parking one at the lower lot and driving to the upper lot to ski down the Powerline, Blacktail Glide, or Z Descent Trails. Do not ski down Blacktail Mountain Road. Traffic can be heavy because of the alpine ski area on the mountain top. The road can get icy.

The 8-mile/13.3-kilometer Powerline Trail takes off from the Alpine Loop at 1.3 miles. The trail casually slopes down, following the powerlines of Blacktail and ending at the Lower Ski Parking Area.

Blacktail Glide begins on Alpine Loop. At 1.3 miles cuts northeast on Powerline. At .9 mile, the Z Descent trail begins heading north. After .4 mile and descending from 4,900 to 4,600 feet, the Blacktail Glide follows the contour of the mountain for a gentler route to the Lower Ski Parking Area. The 7-mile/11.2-kilometer route is groomed as needed and is considered more difficult.

Z Descent is the quickest and steepest route from the Upper Ski Parking Area to the lower area. To reach it, follow the directions to Blacktail Glide. After the first steep downhill, the Z Descent departs down and north, shortcutting 5.8 kilometers off the Blacktail Glide route. The Z Descent provides a great opportunity for telemarking in the clearcut area; however, there are tree stumps either exposed or under the snow. Skiers should use extreme caution in choosing a telemark route through here.

Snowshoers and beginning skiers might try a non-groomed but easy jaunt from the Lower Ski Parking Area. This unnamed route begins at the ski trail but heads northeast along a jeep trail. This is a good choice for kids who may not be able to trek more than a kilometer. The relatively flat and easy terrain travels through the woods but not far from the vehicle.

How to get there

From Kalispell, drive south on U.S. 93 to Lakeside. On the south end of Lakeside and before driving up the big hill, turn right on Blacktail Road. The Lower Ski Parking Area is 6.4 miles from the highway on the left/south at a switchback. The upper parking area is 8.1 miles from the highway on the left/south, at another switchback.

Directions at a glance

The Alpine Loop Trail begins at the southern end of the Upper Ski Parking Area, heading south. Other trails take off from the Alpine Loop. From the Lower Ski Parking Area, trails begin heading south, although it's usually more fun to ski from the upper lot down.

Jewel Basin
Bigfork, Montana

Type of trail:	▬▬ ⬭
Also used by:	Snowmobiles (outside the wilderness boundary)
Distance:	40 miles/64 kilometers
Terrain:	Mountainous
Trail difficulty:	Very challenging climbs and downhills
Surface quality:	Backcountry
Elevation:	3,300 to 7,530 feet
Food and facilities:	Outhouses at the summer trailhead are open in winter but it may be necessary to shovel the snow away from the doors. Remember to bring your own toilet paper. The closest restaurant, the Echo Lake Cafe, is at the junction of Highway 83 and Echo Lake. It's open for breakfast and lunch only. Across the street, the Echo Lake Store has gas and food. Bigfork, 10 miles west, offers all services, including excellent dining at Show Thyme and Tuscany's. There is also a good restaurant at the Mountain Lake Lodge, 5 miles south of Bigfork. A Jewel Basin hiking map can be purchased for a few dollars at the Echo Lake Store or at the Forest Service office or Electric Avenue Books in Bigfork. Backcountry equipment is available in Kalispell at Rocky Mountain Outfitters.
Phone numbers:	U.S. Forest Service (406) 387–3800 or (406) 837–7500. The closest public phones are at the Echo Lake Cafe (406) 837–4254 and Echo Lake Store (406) 837–4727. Bigfork Chamber of Commerce (406) 837–5888. Rocky Mountain Outfitters (406) 752–2446. Avalanche information (406) 257–8402 or in Montana (800) 526–5329. Emergency 911 alerts the sheriff and search and rescue organizations. Cell phones work intermittently here.

Jewel Basin is a 15,000-acre hiking area north of the Bob Marshall Wilderness. No motor vehicles are allowed in Jewel Basin, although snowmobilers utilize the access road and nearby snowmobile trails. Within Jewel Basin are some 35 miles of marked hiking and skiing trails plus the 3- to 6-mile ski-in; however, most climb into the area to telemark, snowboard, or alpine tour. Because the terrain is mountainous, climbing skins and edged skis are necessary. You should also come equipped with avalanche gear, including transceivers, probe poles, and

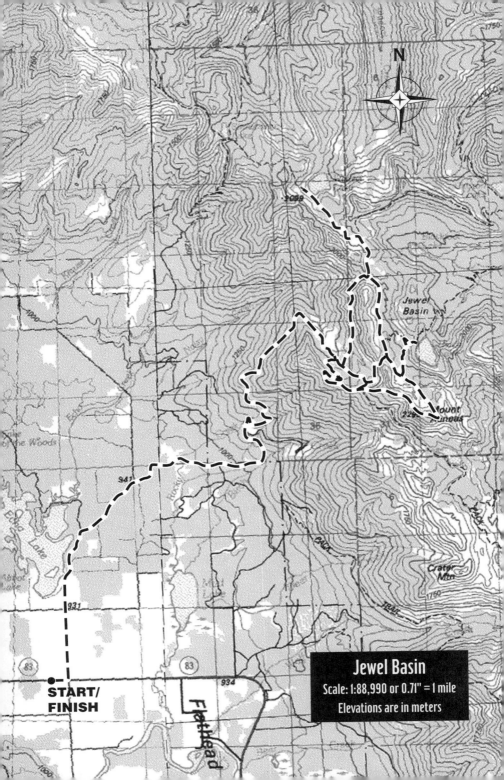

N

Jewel Basin
Scale: 1:88,990 or 0.71" = 1 mile
Elevations are in meters

START/
FINISH

shovels, and be thoroughly familiar with the principles and techniques of avalanche safety. Winter camping is popular in Jewel Basin. Permits are not required; however, campfires are banned from four lakeside campgrounds. Dogs are allowed here but must be leashed at all times.

From the winter parking area, ski east and uphill on Jewel Basin Road 3 to 5 miles (depending on snow line) to the gate for summer parking and trailhead area. This approximately 2,000-foot elevation gain takes a few sweaty hours. Many skiers plan ahead to catch a snowmobile ride up to the Jewel Basin parking area. From here, several routes are available.

The ridge climb to the top of Mount Aeneas at 7,528 feet offers great views of the Flathead Valley and telemark slopes for the route back down. From Camp Misery at 5,717 feet skiers take Trail 717, which leaves the gate heading west. (Don't confuse this with the Trail 8 trailhead, which leaves to the left of the cabin heading north.) Three switchbacks and 1.4 miles later is a trail junction. Remain on Trail 717, the middle trail, heading east. A half mile farther is the microwave tower. Stay on the trail for another .5 mile to the ridge that leads to the summit of Mt. Aeneas. Leave the trail following the ridge line. Telemarking back down the saddle is easiest. After fresh snow, snowboarders' tracks ripple the mountain. The slopes of Mount Aeneas are fun but prone to avalanche.

The ski loop to the Picnic Lakes continues on Trail 717 about 1.5 miles past the ridge climb to Mount Aeneas. One popular option is to continue north past Picnic Lakes on Trail 392 and ski the bowl into Black Lake. Other options connect with Twin Lakes and Wildcat Lakes on Trail 7 (see map). The return trip can either retrace the route past Mount Aeneas or make a loop via Trail 392 northwest from Picnic Lakes .3 mile to Trail 7 and up and over the crest to a challenging downhill. Watch for avalanche danger. The trail descends to meet with Trail 68. Skiers can take 68 heading north to meet with Trail 8, turn left/southwest, and go a final .7 mile to Camp Misery. The other option is to take Trail 7 south, which meets up with Trail 717. Take Trail 717 left/north and go 1.4 miles west before skiing the switchbacks to the gate.

The ski out—down the road—is fast, so remember to take a dry hat, dry shirt, and dry gloves for the chill.

An alternative trail for a winter walk, ski, or snowshoe is the 4-mile round trip on the Swan River Nature Trail in Bigfork. From downtown Bigfork, drive Electric Avenue north to the T with Grand Avenue. Turn east on Grand and drive up the hill. Grand Avenue dead ends at the Swan River Nature Trail. The trailhead sign is located at the east end of the parking area. The gentle trail follows along the north side of the Swan

River through a wooded easement on a closed road. After the first mile, the terrain opens up and offers vistas of the surrounding peaks. The trail gains a few feet in elevation.

How to get there

Two miles north of Bigfork is the junction of Highways 35 and 83. Take Highway 83 going east 2.7 miles. At the Echo Lake Cafe, turn left/north on Echo Lake Road. After 1 mile, stay to the right at a Y, which becomes Foothills Drive. Continue 2 miles to Jewel Basin Road/Forest Road #5392, (also known as Noisy Creek Road). Turn right/east at the small, arrow-shaped sign for Jewel Basin. Park where the road is no longer passable.

Holland Lake

Condon, Montana

Type of trail:	▬▬ ⬬
Also used by:	Snowmobilers
Distance:	6.2 miles/10 kilometers groomed, plus 25 miles backcountry
Terrain:	Flat to mountainous
Trail difficulty:	Easy groomed routes to expert off-piste
Surface quality:	Machine-groomed intermittently and skier-tracked
Elevation:	4,030 to 7,500 feet
Food and facilities:	Holland Lake Lodge offers cozy cabins and a lodge on the shore of Holland Lake. The adjacent Forest Service campground is closed in winter but provides nice picnicking spots. Holland Lake Lodge's excellent dining room is open winter weekends and weekdays for groups with reservations. Limited food, lodging, grocery, and gas services are in nearby Condon, on Highway 83, 12 miles north of the Holland Lake turnoff. Locals suggest the Hungry Bear steakhouse or Montana Charlie's for Italian fare. The lodge has limited snowshoe and ski rentals. Equipment is available at the Seeley Lake Fun Center (406) 677–2287 and in Kalispell at the Sportsman Ski Haus and Rocky Mountain Outfitters.
Phone numbers:	Holland Lake Lodge (406) 754–2282. Super 8 Lodge in Condon (406) 754–2688. Flathead National Forest (406) 755–5401. Swan Lake Ranger District (406) 837–7500. Seeley Lake Fun Center (406) 677–2287. Sportsman Ski Haus (406) 755–6486. Rocky Mountain Outfitters (406) 752–2446.

The Holland Lake area is a quiet winter spot under the Swan Mountains. A guest facility since 1924, it burned and was rebuilt in 1947. The cozy log and timber building houses an excellent restaurant, bar, and a few hotel rooms. Rustic cabins among tall timbers look out on Holland Lake, Holland Falls, and the Swan Mountain Range. The peaks of the Swan Range jet upward from the far shore to 9,000 and 10,000 feet. The crest of the Swan Range borders the rugged Bob Marshall Wilderness. Other activities include ice skating, ice fishing for cutthroat and kokanee salmon, and visiting the tame bobcat named, of course, Bobbie.

The trailhead for both the groomed trails and backcountry routes begins near the lodge parking area at the corral and trail sign. Green, diamond-shaped markers keep skiers on trails, and no trail fee is charged.

Skiers can choose from four different groomed trails, including the

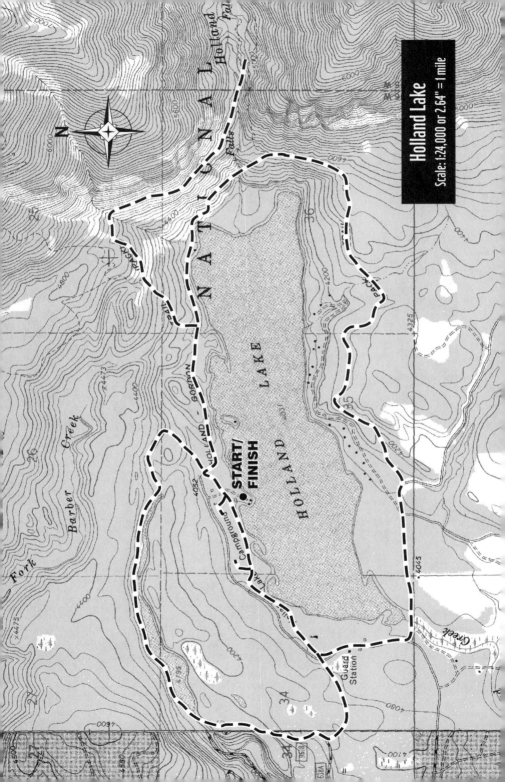

Holland Lake
Scale: 1:24,000 or 2.64" = 1 mile

START/
FINISH

NATIONAL

HOLLAND LAKE

Campground

Guard
Station

favorite beginner 1-kilometer Bay Loop. The trail starts at the barn area heading southwest on the Lakeshore Trail for .5 kilometer. Skiers turn right/northwest for a loop through the campground's ponderosa pine, tamarack, and Douglas fir trees. Kids like the gentle route, where they can find rabbit and deer tracks. The Larch Loop, another beginner 1-kilometer route, is farther along the Lakeshore Trail south of the Bay Loop. It offers similar terrain mostly among larch trees.

For a longer route, skiers continue southwest on the 3-kilometer Lakeshore Trail for 2.5 kilometers, where the trail turns northwest just before Owl Packer Road. Skiers can either retrace their tracks back to the lodge or cross Holland Lake Road where it intersects with Owl Packer Road (watch out for snowmobiles). After crossing Holland Lake Road, the trail becomes the 5-kilometer Eagle Crest Trail. Eagle Crest climbs about 200 feet to a small ridge that provides views of the lake and mountains. Eagle Crest travels north to the lodge and should be skied in this direction because the few switchbacks near the trail's end are recommended for downhill rather than uphill travel.

The 7-mile ski on the snow-covered ice around 416-acre Holland Lake is a popular route. Before going out onto the ice, check with the lodge or the Swan Lake Ranger District office for ice thickness and safety. A skier-packed trail often wraps around the shoreline. Use caution at the lake outlet near the campground, where unreliable ice makes it prudent to ski on the shore.

A more challenging trail begins with a ski around the lake to its northeast corner, and then onto Holland Falls Trail #416. The 3-mile round-trip trail can be icy and in some conditions is better suited to snowshoes or skis with climbing skins. From the trailhead, follow skier-made tracks northeast on the road from the lodge. The road dead ends .5 mile east of the lodge, where the Holland Falls Trail begins heading east along the lake's shoreline. At the northeast corner of the lake, the trail climbs a talus slope, which in the winter is often icy. The steady climb makes two switchbacks before arriving at the frozen falls.

A popular backcountry trail is the Holland Gordon Trail #35 from the lake, climbing 9 miles to Gordon Pass at 7,500 feet. By summer, this trail fills with horse packers headed into the Bob Marshall Wilderness. In winter, snowmobiles pack the route on weekends. From the lodge, ski south around the lake to the southeast shore. Look for the sign for Packer Camp across the road, about 150 yards from the lake. The trailhead is across the road from the entrance to Packer Camp. It's in the woods and marked with a wooden sign. Winter campers utilize a high-mountain meadow below the pass for camping. Avalanche danger is high above the tree line.

Directions at a glance

Trails depart from the paddock area. From the parking lot, walk north-west toward the road 200 feet. Look for the groomed tracks at the paddock. Ski south along the groomed route.

How to get there

Holland Lake is 1.6 miles from Highway 83, 75 miles south of Kalispell and 75 miles northeast of Missoula. Highway 83, the Seeley-Swan Highway, is well known as a wildlife corridor. Drivers should use extreme caution day and night both for potentially icy conditions and for deer on the highway. Eagles and other birds feed on road kills along the shoulder. Watch for snowmobiles on adjacent roads and highway shoulders.

From Highway 83, the turnoff to Holland Lake is 12 miles south of Condon at the large wooden sign for the lodge. The sign is most visible to southbound travelers. Turn east on Holland Lake Road and drive 2.6 miles. The road splits. Keep to the left/north and continue 1.6 miles to the driveway into the lodge. Turn right at the paddock and drive toward the lake.

Seeley Creek Nordic Ski Trails

Seeley Lake, Montana

Type of trail: ▬ ◄

Also used by: There are adjacent trail systems for snowmobiles and dogsleds, which stay off the ski trails.

Distance: 11 miles/18 kilometers

Terrain: Rolling hills

Trail difficulty: Easy to more difficult

Surface quality: Machine-groomed weekly

Elevation: 4,150 to 4,400 feet

Food and facilities: There is an outhouse but no running water at the trailhead. Another outhouse and a picnic shelter with fire pits is across the road at the snowmobile and dogsled parking area. The town of Seeley Lake is a mile from the trailhead and offers all services. Seeley Lake hotels can fill with snowmobilers on weekends so reservations are suggested. The Chamber of Commerce lists several lodging facilities. The two more comfortable lodgings are the Double Arrow Resort, 2 miles south of town, and The Emily A. Bed & Breakfast, 5 miles north of town. Seeley has several cafes and bars. Locals suggest the Double Arrow Resort's gourmet dining room, Lindey's Prime Steak, Double Front Chicken, and the Filling Station . The Seeley Lake Fun Center rents ski equipment.

Phone numbers: Seeley Lake Ranger Station (406) 677–2233. Seeley Chamber of Commerce (406) 677–2880. Double Arrow Resort (800) 468–0777 or (406) 677–2777. The Emily A. Bed & Breakfast (800) 977–4639 or (406) 677–3474. Seeley Lake Fun Center (406) 677–2287. Avalanche advisory (800) 526–5329. Emergency 911. Road report (800) 332–6171.

The Seeley Creek trail system is a challenging, well-maintained, and well-marked set of classic and skate lanes at the base of the Swan Mountain Range. It has evolved from a primitive trail system, constructed in the 1970s, to a finely tuned ski center that draws dozens of marathon ski racers to the annual O.S.C.R. 50-kilometer race on the last Saturday in January. The nearby community of Seeley Lake is popular with snowmobilers, who have 300 miles of groomed sled routes of their own. Dog sledders have yet another set of trails that depart from the nearby trailhead. The mid-winter snow depth averages about 3 feet in the Seeley-Swan Valley, which is 80 miles long, 30 miles wide, and bordered by wilderness on two sides.

From the trailhead, all skiers begin on the Logging Camp Loop heading north. Logging Camp is named for a 1920s-era log campsite, still visible in summer. Note that most loops travel in a clockwise direction. Trails and junctions are well marked. This rolling route through tamarack trees and small meadows switches back after .8 kilometer. First-time skiers should turn back at the first intersection, taking the right/east route for a .9-kilometer return ski. Novices opting for a 2.9-kilometer total can continue northeast at this junction and take the Bull Pine Loop. At the next junction, .4 kilometer farther, Bull Pine skiers turn right/north for .2-kilometer uphill and then another right/east and uphill to complete the 1.2-kilometer Bull Pine Loop. The return to the trailhead on Logging Camp is .9 kilometer.

Other routes take off from the Bull Pine Loop, including Two Creeks Loop, which crosses creeks on bridges. The very challenging hill routes of Mountain View and Larch Knob provide views of the Swan Range and Crescent, Pyramid, and Morrell Peaks. Roller Coaster, a 2.7-kilometer loop, is just like it sounds, up and down through meadows and forested terrain.

For skiers or snowshoers who want a different adventure, the groomed snowmobile roads are generally quiet during the midweek. The road just past the Seeley Creek Trailhead leads to Morrell Falls. This is a challenging, 17.5-mile round-trip backcountry experience. From the trail-

head, go out on the road to the immediate junction with West Morrell
Road #4353. Turn north and follow the road 6 miles. Turn east on Pyramid Pass Road #4381 and ski .25 mile. Turn north on Morrell Falls Road
#4364 and ski 1 mile to the Morrell Falls trailhead. The trail climbs 2.5
miles to the falls. Morrell Falls is a series of waterfalls and cascades,
mostly frozen in winter. The largest falls is at the bottom and is about 90
vertical feet.

Guests and visitors at Double Arrow Resort can test their wax on the
2-mile groomed trail that laces through the ranch's meadows. Aside from
this beginner jaunt, the ranch has 200 acres to explore on snowshoe or
ski, or aboard the horse-drawn sleigh, but watch out for snowmobiles.

How to get there

Seeley Lake is on Highway 83, 90 miles south of Kalispell and 45
miles northeast of Missoula. Highway 83, the Seeley-Swan Highway, is
well known as a wildlife corridor. Drivers should use extreme caution
day and night, and be on the lookout for deer on the highway or eagles
and other birds feeding on road kills. This highway is often covered with
snow and ice. Snowmobilers may be jetting along adjacent roads or highway shoulders.

From the highway, turn east on Morrell Creek Road, which locals call
Cottonwood Lakes Road/FS Rd. #477. If deep snow covers the signs,
look for the hand-made sign for the Wolf Ridge Apartments at mile
marker 15. Drive 1.1 miles, staying on the main road. The ski trailhead is
on the left/north and immediately across from the snowmobile/dogsled
trailhead on the right/south.

Garnet Ghost Town
Missoula, Montana

Type of trail:	▬▬▬ ⬤⬤⬤⬤
Also used by:	Snowmobilers
Distance:	6-mile/9.5-kilometer round trip into Garnet; 3 miles/5 kilometers of skier-only trails; 116 miles/186 kilometers of multiple-use trails
Terrain:	Some flats but mostly hilly
Trail difficulty:	Easy to more difficult
Surface quality:	Groomed as needed and some skier-tracked trails
Elevation:	4,500 to 7,000 feet
Food and facilities:	There are no facilities at the trailhead. A frost-free hydrant remains open in winter for good water in Garnet. No services are open in this ghost town unless visitors have made reservations to stay in one of the very rustic rental cabins. One rental, the Dahl cabin, which sleeps eight, was built in 1932, and was originally a speakeasy complete with bar, poker tables, and slot machines. All services are available in Missoula, including equipment retailers Bob Ward & Sons, the Army & Navy Economy Store, The Trailhead, Pipestone Mountaineering, and Gart Sports.
Phone numbers:	The Bureau of Land Management (406) 329–3914 has information on trail conditions. Cabin reservations (406) 329–1031. There are no phones in Garnet Ghost Town, but a full-time caretaker lives in one of the cabins and has emergency-only radio contact with the BLM offices. Cell phones do work from some places along the ski trails. Emergency 911 contacts the sheriffs' offices. Because borders of three counties meet near Garnet, emergencies are handled by the Missoula County Sheriff (406) 721–5700, the Granite County Sheriff (406) 859–3251, and the Powell County Sheriff (406) 846–2711.

Garnet Ghost Town in the Garnet Mountain Range is among the more unusual and unknown ski sites in the West. Not only do skiers find remnants of the West's wild past, they can stay the night in either of two rustic cabins available for rent in Garnet. Garnet sits at the 6,000-foot elevation and generally has good snow from early winter to early spring.

The Garnet caretaker grooms the cross-country routes and can suggest the best routes for the day's conditions. Most trails are groomed for multiple use and can be very busy with weekend snowmobilers. The BLM suggests that when skiers hear snowmobilers on the trail, the skiers should step off the trail until the machines pass.

The ski into Garnet is a pleasant day trip, with a choice of either 6 or 8 miles round trip. Skiers could take the easier and longer Cave Gulch Trail in and the swifter Bear Gulch Trail out for a 7-mile round trip. Both

trails begin at the Beartown parking area, and both gain 1,500 feet in elevation to the ghost town. Skiers should be prepared to shed layers of clothing. The Bear Gulch Trail travels the "Chinee" Grade, where a Chinese miner reportedly buried his fortune in a baking-powder can a century ago—it was never found! About a quarter mile from the parking area the Cave Gulch Trail takes off to the right and gently climbs through forested hills to meet up with the Summit Cabin Loop Trail. Neither trail is steep enough to require climbing skins in most snow conditions, although skins might be useful if the conditions become extremely icy.

The 8.8-mile/15-kilometer loop trail up to Summit Cabin, now a dilapidated log pile, is a scenic tour that passes Reynolds City, another former mining town. The trail has gentle to moderate hills, dropping down to about 5,600 feet and climbing to 6,300 feet. This loop trail begins at Garnet Ghost Town, travels north .7 mile, turns right/east to Elk Creek Summit, then down the Elk Creek Road for 2.9 miles to a junction with the Garnet Range Road. About a mile after this junction is Reynolds City ghost town but there isn't much of it left to see. Skiers remain on the right hand route 5.6 miles from the junction back to Garnet. Several historic mines and cabins are on private property and present hazards if climbed on. The Summit Cabin is about 1.5 miles before Garnet.

Garnet Ghost Town

Scale: 1:34,780 or 1.82" = 1 mile

START/FINISH

Directions at a glance

The route begins at the Beartown parking area. Look for the trailhead sign on the northern edge of the parking area. The easier, 4-mile Cave Gulch Trail leaves Bear Gulch Trail at .25 mile, turning right, and climbs to Summit Cabin Loop Trail. At this junction, turn left/west and ski about 1.6 kilometers to Garnet. Skiers can return via the shorter and steeper 5-kilometer Bear Gulch Trail from Garnet, leaving Garnet heading south on Bear Gulch Trail to the trailhead. Both the Cave Gulch and Bear Gulch routes are groomed and used by snowmobilers. There are signs at the trail junctions.

Additional loop trails take off from the Summit Cabin Loop Trail, including the 3.4-mile Top O'Deep Loop. Maps available from the BLM office.

While Garnet is refreshingly uncommercialized, overnighters must remember that they need to carry in all their food and carry out all their trash. Running water is available from a hand pump near the Dahl cabin. Outhouses are a few steps away from "downtown."

Be alert when skiing in any former mining area. Open mine shafts may be partially or entirely obscured by snow. The open mine shafts are extremely hazardous. This area is not patrolled, so for your safety, the BLM advises that you stay on the trails and roads.

How to get there

To access the Beartown trailhead drive 42 miles from Missoula along I-90. Take the Bearmouth exit north and following Old Highway 10 to Bear Gulch Road. Drive north 8 miles to the Beartown trailhead, staying on the plowed road. Park in the plowed area.

Rattlesnake Recreation Area/ Rattlesnake Wilderness/Patti Canyon

Missoula, Montana

Type of trail:	▬▬▬ ⬭
Also used by:	Hikers
Distance:	20 miles/32 kilometers
Terrain:	Gentle elevation gain to expert backcountry
Trail difficulty:	Easy to very difficult
Surface quality:	Skier-tracked but often walked on by hikers and joggers, especially within the first 3 kilometers from the trailhead
Elevation:	3,860 to 7,960 feet
Food and facilities:	Missoula offers dozens of lodging and eating possibilities. The Creekside Inn and Goldsmith's Inn are near the trailheads. C'mon Inn is a new lodging facility near I–90 with easy access to trailheads. There is a restroom at the trailhead. Equipment is available in Missoula at Bob Ward & Sons, Open Road Nordic, the Army & Navy Economy Store, The Trailhead, and Pipestone Mountaineering.
Phone numbers:	Missoula Chamber of Commerce (406) 543–6623 or (800) 526–3465. Missoula Ranger District (406) 329–3814. Goldsmith's Inn (406) 721–6732. Creekside Inn (800) 551–2387. C'mon Inn (888) 989–5569. Avalanche information (406) 549–4488. Emergency 911. Cell phones work intermittently in the mountains.

Rattlesnake is an intimidating name, but according to local U.S. Forest Service officials, no rattlesnakes shimmy along the route. The name, it seems, dates back to the early days of Missoula when someone found a rattler, yet the source of the anecdote eludes local historians. Closest to Missoula is the Rattlesnake Recreation Area, 5 miles north of downtown Missoula. Three miles north into the Recreation Area is the boundary of the 33,000-acre Rattlesnake Wilderness. Camping is prohibited within 3 miles of the trailhead.

Spring Gulch Trail is an easy 7-mile round trip in the very popular Rattlesnake Recreation Area. At .5 mile is the Spring Gulch Trail junction. Turn left/northwest and ski on the old road or the paralleling trail 3 miles. Return trips are on the same routes. Beginners might rest and turn around at the old homestead that is in the meadow at the 2.5-mile point. Very old apple trees are known to attract black bears and other animals in the

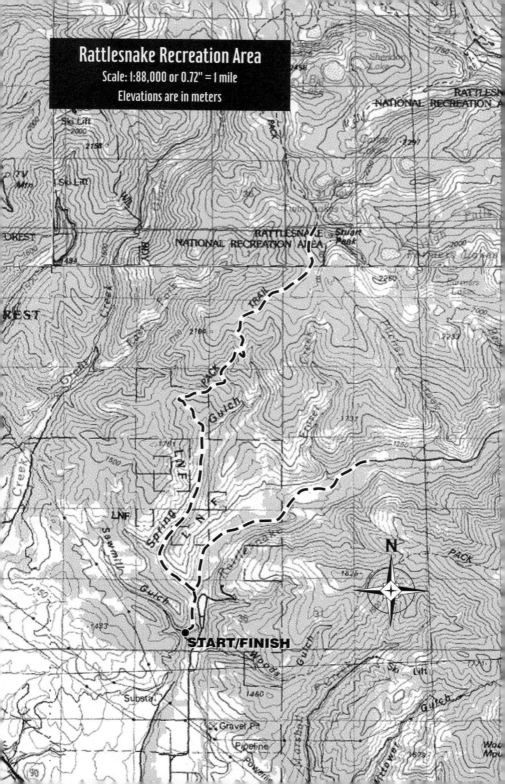

fall. Even in winter, deer and mountain lions frequent the area. The next mile climbs to Kench Meadow on a narrower trail.

After Kench Meadow, the trail climbs and gets more challenging. Most visitors turn around here, but an option for expert backcountry skiers is the climb to Stuart Peak. You can camp overnight at Kench Meadow before attempting the climb, which takes you to the 7,960-foot Stuart Peak over 6.5 miles of avalanche-prone terrain, returning by the same route. The Stuart Peak Trail #517 begins on the left/northwest side of the creek. After 3 miles, the trail enters the Rattlesnake Wilderness. This high alpine lake area includes Twin Lakes, Cliff Lake, and Peterson Lake. There are views of four mountain ranges from the summit of Stuart Peak, including the Bitterroot Mountains to the south, the Mission Mountains north, the Swan Range to the northeast, and the Rockies beyond. Telemarkers and alpine touring skiers will find numerous opportunities for powder skiing; however, this is avalanche territory. Backcountry users on the Stuart Peak Trail should carry avalanche transceivers, probe poles, and shovels—and should know how to use them.

To ski the main Rattlesnake Trail, continue going north at the Spring Gulch Trail junction on the wide jeep/ski trail. The trail crosses into the Rattlesnake Wilderness at 3 miles. This out-and-back ski route continues for 12 miles from the trailhead to the Franklin Bridge.

The groomed Patti Canyon ski trails are a convenient option right on the southeast edge of Missoula. The 9-kilometer Patti Canyon trails are accessed from downtown Missoula via Higgins Street. Go south on Higgins 2 miles (18 blocks) to Patti Canyon Road. Turn left and drive 3 miles up Patti Canyon to the parking area and trailhead. Trails head north or south on either side of road. The north-side, 5-kilometer trails are better for novices. The south side's 4 kilometers are more challenging. Ski trails are well marked and groomed as needed from December through early March for classic and skate skis. Grooming is funded through donations and a donation box is near the trail sign.

How to get there

From downtown Missoula, take Van Buren St. north under the I–90 underpass. Remain on Van Buren staying to the right on what becomes Rattlesnake Drive. Drive north 5 miles. Turn left/west at the signs for the Rattlesnake parking/ trailhead area at Sawmill Gulch.

Patti Canyon trails are accessed from downtown Missoula by driving south on Higgins Avenue for 2 miles. Turn left/uphill on Patti Canyon Road and continue 3 miles up to the parking area.

Directions at a glance

Park in the plowed Rattlesnake parking area. The trail begins at the north end of parking area. Ski around the gate and along the wide trail.

From the Patti Canyon parking area, look for trail signs on both the north and south sides of the parking area, and ski either the easier north-side route or the more challenging south-side route.

Lolo Pass
Lolo, Montana

Type of trail: ▬▬ ⬤

Also used by: Snowboarders and telemarkers; there are snowmobilers on some well-marked, shared-use trails. No dogs allowed.

Distance: 48 miles/77 kilometers

Terrain: Flat meadows, some hilly routes through woods, and mountainous telemark slopes

Trail difficulty: Beginner and intermediate touring; advanced to expert telemarking, snowboarding, and off-track skiing; advanced snowshoeing

Surface quality: Weekend grooming on 8 miles/15 kilometers of single track; other trails are skier-packed. Skating sometimes midweek on snowmobile trails.

Elevation: 5,333 to 5,600 feet, option down to 4,600 feet

Food and facilities: The Lolo Pass Visitor Center and the Warming Hut are open from 9:30 A.M. to 5:30 P.M., Friday through Monday. The log Warming Hut sells the required parking permit for $5 per day or $20 per season. Lolo Hot Springs Resort (800) 273–2290, 7 miles east, offers lodging, a restaurant, bar, and two hot-springs pools. On the Idaho side of Lolo Pass, 13 miles west on Highway 12, is the Lochsa Lodge with cabins, restaurant, bar, gas, and a convenience store. Missoula, 45 miles northeast, has all services. Equipment is available in Missoula at Bob Ward & Sons, Open Road Nordic, the Army & Navy Economy Store, The Trailhead, Pipestone Mountaineering, and Gart Sports.

Phone numbers: Powell Ranger Station at (208) 942–3113 has information on trail conditions. There are no telephones at Lolo Pass. In case of emergency, contact the volunteer in the Warming Hut, who uses a radio to contact the Powell Ranger Station. At night, after the Warming Hut closes, the nearest phone is at the Lolo Hot Springs Resort, 7 miles east of the pass. Cell phones do not usually work from Lolo Pass. Avalanche information (406) 549–4488.

Lolo Pass is in the Bitterroot Mountains, a mountain range 470 miles long. The peaks are 6,000 to 7,000 feet high, with thick, timbered habitat that is home to elk and other wildlife. Lolo Pass carries great historic significance for the Nez Perce Indians, who frequented this route through the mountains from Idaho to their hunting grounds on Montana's plains.

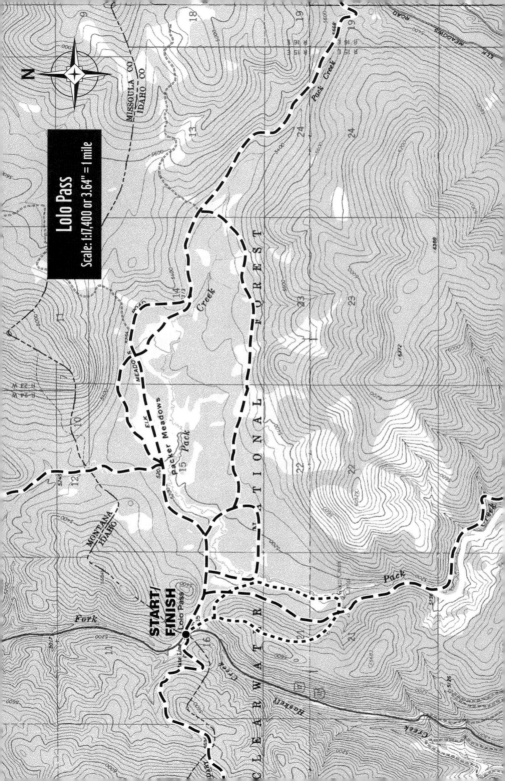

Lolo Pass

Scale: 1:17,400 or 3.64" = 1 mile

N

MISSOULA CO.
IDAHO CO.

MONTANA
IDAHO

Pack Creek

Creek

ELK MEADOWS

Packer Meadows

CLEARWATER NATIONAL FOREST

Pack

START/
FINISH
Lolo Pass

Fork

Creek

Pack

Western Creek

Creek

The Lewis and Clark Corps of Discovery camped here in 1805 en route to the Pacific Ocean. Today the pass is a popular ski and snowshoe route astride the Montana–Idaho border. Ski trails travel both states.

All trails leave from the parking lot, including the 3-mile Dennis E. Elliott Memorial Snowshoe Trail. This steep-climbing and physically strenuous trail loops through a beautiful stand of larch trees, travels up to a ridge top, and then back to the Warming Hut. The elevation gain is approximately 400 feet.

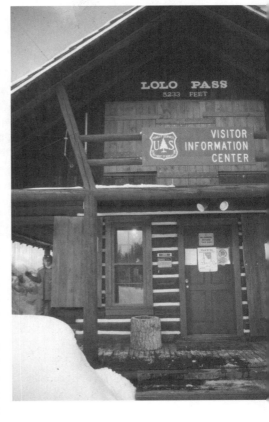

The most popular groomed ski touring trail is the Packer Meadows Loop Trail. The 6-mile loop begins at the Warming Hut, travels east .5 mile to the trail sign at Packer Meadows Loop, and returns on the Elk Meadows Road. Watch for snowshoe hares along this route. The Packer Meadows and other open areas offer off-track skiing on mild slopes for novices. Use caution when venturing off the groomed trails. Small streams meander through the meadows and may not be visible or may not be completely covered by snow.

The Lee Creek Trails are skier-tracked. Both are full-day round-trip routes. From the Visitor Center, follow the Packer Meadows Loop for 1 mile. Look for the Lee Creek sign and trailhead on the north side of the trail. It is a well-marked, skier-only route. The Lee Creek Trail travels north across the state line into Montana and descends to 4,333 feet. At 1.3 miles, the trail splits into Lee Creek A Trail and B Trail. The A Trail is a 6.6-mile more difficult route to the Lee Creek Campground. The B Trail to Wagon Mountain is rated most difficult for the 7 miles, also ending at Lee Creek Campground. There are no services, water, or shelter at the campground.

Snowboarders have recently discovered what telemarkers knew for years, that the 6,052-foot Mt. Fuji offers outstanding powder turns.

Directions at a glance

Park in the plowed Lolo Pass parking lot only. All trails begin at the Warming Hut at the southeast end of the parking area. Do not park on the highway shoulder because the snow plows frequent the highway and will either have the vehicle towed or plow it under.

Be sure to purchase a parking permit and place it in vehicle as directed. Pick up a map in the Visitor Center.

Skiers begin on the Packer Meadows Trail, skiing along the meadows about 1.25 miles before turning south on Glade Creek Loop. The Mt. Fuji Loop turns south from the Glade Creek Loop after .5 mile. The base of Mt. Fuji is 1 mile along the Mt. Fuji Loop Trail. Ski along the 1.3-mile Mt. Fuji Loop and pick a good telemark slope. To return to the parking area, continue on the Mt. Fuji Loop, which returns to Glade Creek Loop. Neither snowboarders on foot nor snowshoers are allowed on the groomed cross-country ski trails. Best bet is to walk or snowshoe next to the snowmobile-groomed Pack Creek Road, 1.5 miles to Fuji's base. Another option for snowboarders is to walk alongside the Glade Creek Loop skier-only trail 1 mile to the base of Fuji. From the base of the mountain, skiers, snowshoers, and boarders climb a variety of routes and schuss the powder. This is avalanche territory. Skiers and boarders accessing Mt. Fuji should carry avalanche transceivers, probes, and shovels, and should know how to use them.

An interesting ski-and-stay alternative is the nearby ski route into the West Fork Butte Lookout which is available for winter nightly rental. The 6.3-mile/10-kilometer route from Elk Meadows is a strenuous climb of 1,174 meters in elevation. The pay off includes several scenic vantage points, and of course a night or two staying in the backcountry. The Missoula Ranger District office has maps, directions and takes reservations at (406) 329–3750. Reservations are absolutely necessary because the lookout is locked.

How to get there

From Missoula take U.S. Highway 93 South 12 miles to the town of Lolo. Turn right/west on U.S. Highway 12 toward Idaho and Lolo Pass. Much of the 33 miles to the pass is windy and can be very slippery in winter so drive cautiously. Watch for logging trucks. At the summit, turn left into the Lolo Pass parking area.

Chief Joseph Cross-Country Ski Trails
Darby, Montana

Type of trail: ▬▬

Also used by: Skiers only

Distance: 14.75 miles/24.6 kilometers

Terrain: Hills and meadows

Trail difficulty: Easiest to more difficult

Surface quality: Machine-groomed weekly

Elevation: 6,800 to 7,420 feet

Food and facilities: The closest restaurant is a mile west at the Lost Trail Ski Area, which is open during the winter from Thursday through Sunday and on holidays. Jackson Hot Springs Lodge, 48 miles east of the pass, is known for gourmet dining in a 1950 log lodge. Cozy cabins are popular on winter weekends so lodging reservations are necessary. The pool at Jackson Hot Springs is a constant 104 degrees F, cooled down from the source at 136 degrees F. Camp Creek Inn Bed & Breakfast is 9 miles north of Lost Trail Pass and offers rooms in a 1919 historic ranch house or in cabins with kitchens. Groceries and gas are available in Wisdom and Darby. There is an outhouse at the trailhead and a proposed warming hut/outhouse planned for a spot on the Picnic Meadow Loop. Ski equipment is available in Hamilton at Bob Ward & Sons, or in Missoula at The Trailhead, Pipestone Mountaineering, and the Bob Ward & Sons store.

Phone numbers: Sula Ranger District (406) 821–3201. Wisdom Ranger District (406) 689–3243. Bitterroot Cross Country Ski Club, P.O. Box 431, Corvallis, MT 59828. Lost Trail Ski Area (406) 821–3211 or (406) 821–3508. Jackson Hot Springs Lodge (406) 834–3151. Camp Creek Inn Bed & Breakfast (406) 821–3508. Avalanche advisory (800) 281–1030. Emergency 911 alerts the sheriff's office

The Chief Joseph Pass Cross-Country Ski Trails are at the confluence of two mountain passes that are significant in Western history. Trails begin at the top of Chief Joseph Pass, next to Lost Trail Pass. Chief Joseph and his band of Nez Perce Indians traveled through this pass in 1877, fleeing U.S. Army troops and the federal government's attempt to place them on an Indian reservation. Their 1,300-mile journey ended just 40 miles short of the Canadian border and freedom. Once they surrendered,

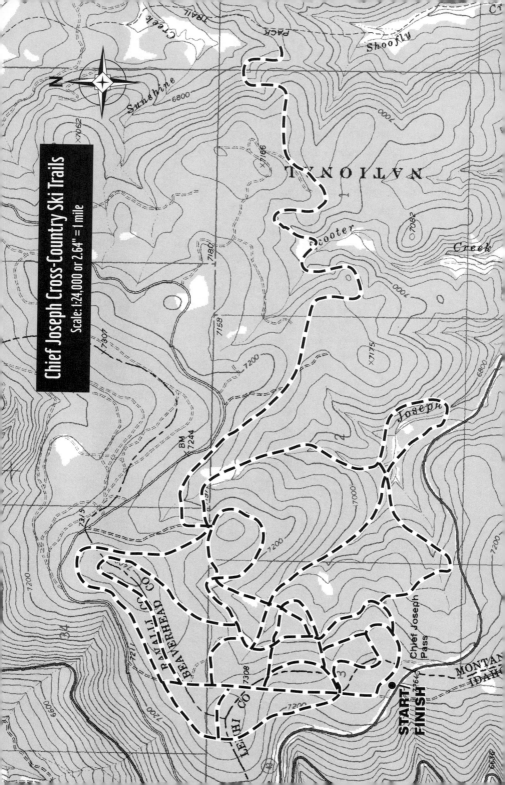

Chief Joseph Cross-Country Ski Trails
Scale: 1:24,000 or 2.64" = 1 mile

they were sent to a reservation in Oklahoma and later one in Washington. Nearby Lost Trail Pass was named by the Lewis and Clark Expedition in 1805, when the expedition was lost and near starvation on its journey to the Pacific Ocean.

The trail system is well maintained by the Bitterroot X-C Ski Club, which asks for donations to groom the trails. There are maps, information, a donation box, and schedules for ski club events and trips at the trailhead. Trails are not groomed for skating and dogs are not allowed. Note that severe winter storms can blow in very suddenly. Skiers should be prepared with layers of clothing, backpack, water, a snack, and a map. The trails are well marked and most are marked for direction. Because the trailhead is at the top of the pass, the trails generally go downhill with a return ski uphill. Be aware that beginner skiers may have difficulty climbing from the low point of 6,800 feet at Lower Loop back up to the summit.

From the trailhead, begin skiing east on a short trail that accesses the rest of the trail system. The first loop, Sunny Meadow Loop, is an easy 1.8 kilometers and is appropriate for beginners. Kids and telemarkers like the more difficult 2.5-kilometer Picnic Meadow Loop. Ski from the trailhead to the Picnic Meadow Loop following the trail's suggested direction. Look east into the Big Hole Valley. At the meadow, telemarkers' tracks lace the slope. Kids find jumps (and crashes) in the snow drifts here. Skiers can continue on Picnic Meadow Loop to the CD Trail and return to the trailhead or choose from numerous other loops before returning to the trailhead. There are views east to the alpine ski area of Lost Trail Powder Mountain and toward the North Fork of the Salmon River in Idaho.

For a longer day ski, take the first right/east turn off the Sunny Meadow Loop onto the Banshee Trail heading east and downhill for 1.8 kilometers. This trail descends 315 feet through five small meadows before crossing the west fork of Joseph Creek. Dense forests and small natural meadows dominate the scenery of the Banshee Trail. Banshee meets up at The Forks with Lower Loop and the lowest elevation on the trail system. Continue east and then southeast on Joseph Creek/Lower Loop for 1.2 kilometers. Just before the trail loops back, there is a marked emergency trail exit to the highway. Stay on the trail, loop back north, and keep right at the junction to ski the 2.4-kilometer Middle Fork Trail. Middle Fork climbs up from Joseph Creek through dense forest and open meadows.

Another beginner trail is the 2-kilometer Continental Divide Trail, which is marked on the signs as CD Trail. This can be skied out and back from the trailhead. Begin to the left/northwest at the trailhead, ski around the parking area, and then head north on a wide thoroughfare. Several trails take off from or end at the CD Trail.

HowTo Get There

From Missoula, drive south on Highway 93 for 90 miles to Lost Trail Pass. The pass is 10 miles south of the Sula Ranger Station. At the summit, turn left/east on Highway 43 for 1 mile. Turn left/ north into the parking area. If the snow is deep the sign may be buried, so look for the snow-depth measurement sign on the highway's north side—it's right at the entrance to the parking area.

Directions at a glance

From the middle of the large parking area, all trails begin on the northeast side between the outhouse and the trailhead sign. Climb the bank and ski northeast.

North Big Hole/Saddle Mountain Trails
Darby, Montana

Type of trail:	▬▬ ⬭
Also used by:	Alpine touring skiers, telemarkers, and snowmobilers
Distance:	31.75 miles/51.2 kilometers
Terrain:	Mountainous
Trail difficulty:	More difficult to expert backcountry
Surface quality:	Skier-tracked backcountry
Elevation:	6,400 to 8,039 feet
Food and facilities:	An outhouse at the Chief Joseph trailhead parking is open and maintained year round. Lost Trail Powder Mountain Ski Area does not rent cross-country equipment but the food service is open Thursday through Sunday and holidays. Skiers can buy a one-ride lift ticket to access some Saddle Mountain trails. Jackson Hot Springs Lodge, 48 miles east of the pass, is known for gourmet dining in a 1950 log lodge. Cozy cabins are popular on winter weekends so lodging reservations are necessary. Jackson Hot Springs' pool is a constant 104 degrees F, cooled down from the source at 136 degrees F. Camp Creek Inn Bed & Breakfast is 9 miles north of Lost Trail Pass and offers rooms in a 1919 historic ranch house or in cabins with kitchens. Triple Creek Ranch Restaurant near Darby has gourmet food, reservations necessary. Groceries and gas are available in Wisdom and Darby. Ski equipment is available in Hamilton at Bob Ward & Sons, or in Missoula at The Trailhead, Pipestone Mountaineering, and Bob Ward & Sons.
Phone numbers:	Sula Ranger District (406) 821–3201. Wisdom Ranger District (406) 689–3243. Bitterroot Cross Country Ski Club, P.O. Box 431, Corvallis, MT 59828. Lost Trail Ski Area (406) 821–3211 or (406) 821–3508. Jackson Hot Springs Lodge (406) 834–3151. Camp Creek Inn Bed & Breakfast (406) 821–3508. Triple Creek Ranch Restaurant (406) 821–4664. Avalanche advisory (800) 281–1030 or (406) 587–6981. Emergency 911 alerts the sheriff's office.

The North Big Hole is named for the Big Hole River, which flows east from Chief Joseph Pass into the grand Big Hole Valley, the "land of 10,000 hay bales." In the 1800s, the Big Hole Basin was along a well-known fur-trading route that included several "holes," or valleys. Ranchers first

North Big Hole/Saddle Mountain Trails
Scale: 1:77,520 or 0.82" = 1 mile
Elevations are in meters

grazed livestock in the 1870s because of the 125 varieties of wild grasses. The Big Hole is home to only a few hundred people in small towns like Jackson, with a population of fifty people—and sixty dogs. Nearby Saddle Mountain trailheads are on Lost Trail Pass, named by the Lewis and Clark Expedition when they became lost here en route to the Pacific in 1805.

The ungroomed trails offer backcountry skiers days on different trails. Controlled dogs are permitted on the trails. Weather blows in quickly. Backcountry travelers use skis with metal edges and carry packs with extra clothing, food, and survival gear. Skiers should understand avalanche hazards, have route-finding skills, and be able to ski in white-out conditions. Good maps are available from the Forest Service offices in Sula and Wisdom.

Eight different trails comprise the North Big Hole system, a combination of logging roads and single-track trail. Among the most popular is the Anderson Mountain Road Trail, which begins across Highway 43 from the Chief Joseph Pass Cross-Country Ski Trails parking area. Use caution when walking south across the highway to the Anderson trailhead. The trail begins heading south and downhill into a forested area. The trail cruises ups and downs along the Continental Divide, summiting Anderson Mountain at 8,039 feet. Clearcuts provide telemarking opportunities. Blue diamonds on trees mark the trail, which can be very challenging in white-out conditions.

Several trails intersect the Anderson Mountain Road Trail and can be skied either from Anderson or from trailheads along Highway 43. The first intersection is with Richardson Ridge Trail, a most difficult 2.5-mile trail heading east and down to the highway. Ski Anderson Mountain Road Trail 1.25 miles south. Turn left/east on Richardson Ridge Trail and ski 2.5 miles to the highway. Either return along the same route or arrange a shuttle parked in a small pullout on the south side of Highway 43 at mile marker 4 (3 miles east of Chief Joseph Pass).

The Cabinet Creek Trail connects with Anderson 3.8 miles from the pass. Turn east and ski 3 miles to Highway 43. Either retrace your tracks or leave a shuttle vehicle at the Cabinet Creek trailhead at a pullout at mile marker 5. Along the Cabinet Creek Trail is the beginning of May Creek Ridge Trail, a most difficult 5.5-mile route to May Creek Campground. Ax-cut blazes and blue diamonds mark the trail.

The May Creek Trail is also accessed from Cabinet Creek Trail. May Creek is a 6-mile, more difficult route that passes the May Creek Cabin. The upper 3 miles are steep and require the use of edged skis. The lower section is relatively easy terrain. The cabin can be rented through the Wisdom Ranger District. The May Creek trailhead and the May Creek Ridge trailhead begin at mile marker 8 on Highway 43 on the south side of the road, at the May Creek campground.

The Saddle Mountain Road Ski Trail, a 9-kilometer route, begins at the Lost Trail Ski Area on Forest Road #5734 south of the chairlifts. Watch out for alpine skiers on the first mile. The trail cuts back north and down to Lost Trail Hot Springs. A popular alternative begins at the top of Chairlift #1. Skiers purchase a one-ride ticket. From the top of the lift, the trail heads north along the ridge line. Follow the trail down to Lost Trail Hot Springs.

Saddle Mountain Road Trail departs south of the ski area's lifts or from the top of Chairlift #1.

How to get there

Anderson Mountain Road Trail departs directly across Highway 43 from the Chief Joseph Pass Cross-Country Ski Trails parking area. Park in the parking area and use caution when walking south across the highway to the Anderson trailhead.

The Saddle Mountain Road Ski Trail begins at the Lost Trail Ski Area. At the top of Lost Trail Pass, turn west and into the ski area's parking lot.

Directions at a glance

From the Chief Joseph Pass Cross-Country Ski Trails parking area walk south across the highway to the Anderson trailhead.

Big Hole Battlefield
Wisdom, Montana

Type of trail: ▬▬▬ 🌟

Also used by: Moose, elk, and raptors

Distance: 10.5 miles/16.8 kilometers

Terrain: Meadows and hills

Trail difficulty: Easy to moderate

Surface quality: Machine-groomed as needed

Elevation: 6,100 to 6,300 feet

Food and facilities: The Visitor Center at the Big Hole National Battlefield is open daily from 9 A.M. to 5 P.M. and has a museum, rest rooms, and a small gift shop. There are a few snowshoes available to borrow; however, there is no rental ski equipment. Rental skis can be found in Dillon, Butte, Hamilton, and Missoula. The Visitor Center has running water but no food for sale. Picnic tables are available on the trail system. The closest lodging, restaurants, and grocery store are 10 miles east in Wisdom. Restaurants include The Big Hole Crossing, Fetty's Cafe, and the Antler Saloon, which has pizza. There are two small motels in Wisdom. The Jackson Hot Springs Lodge, on Highway 278, 18 miles south of Wisdom, offers soaks in the 104-degree hot springs pool, lodging, a gourmet restaurant, and bar. More accommodations are available at Lost Trail Pass and in Dillon, Butte, Hamilton, and Missoula. The closest airports are Butte, 75 miles northeast, and Missoula, 110 miles north. No public transportation is available. Winter travelers should use 4-wheel-drive vehicles in this snow-belt region.

Phone numbers: Big Hole National Battlefield (406) 689–3155. Travel information in the region (800) 879–1159 or (406) 846–1943. Nez Perce Motel (406) 689–3254. Sandman Motel (406) 689–3218. Jackson Hot Springs Lodge (406) 834–3151. Wisdom Ranger District (406) 689–3243. Avalanche information (800) 281–1030 or (406) 587–6981. Emergency 911. There is an outside pay phone at the Visitor Center. Cell phones work intermittently.

The 655-acre Big Hole National Battlefield site honors the Nez Perce, U.S. 7th Infantry soldiers, and Bitterroot Volunteers who died here on August 9–10, 1877. An estimated ninety Nez Perce men, women, and

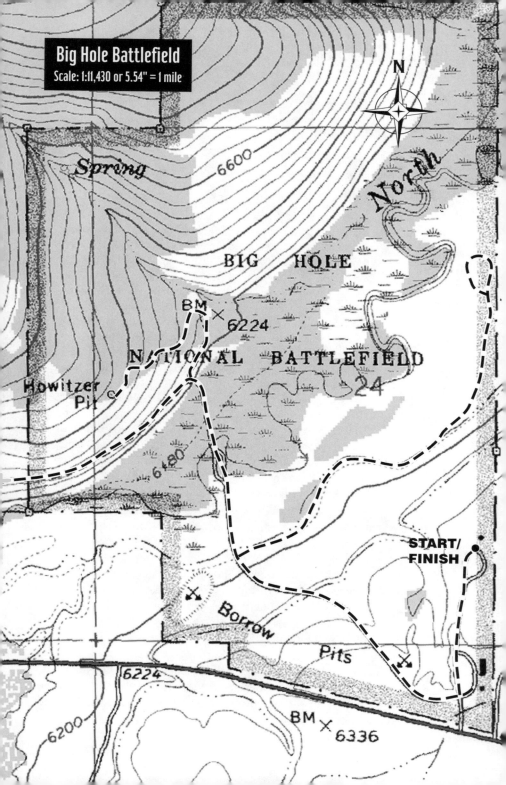

children, as well as thirty-one soldiers and volunteers, perished in the fighting. Because miners, settlers, and stockmen encroached on traditional Nez Perce lands of Oregon and Idaho, 800 Nez Perce fled before the army could force them onto a reservation. Their 1,300-mile flight included several battles in which the Indians were led by Chief Looking Glass. The chase culminated about 700 miles from here, with the surrender of the Nez Perce near Montana's Bears Paw Mountains, 40 miles short of the Canadian border and freedom. It is from the Bears Paws that Chief Joseph's famous words echo: "From where the sun now stands, I will fight no more forever."

The National Park Service reminds visitors that the Nez Perce consider this a sacred place. The Nez Perce who fell that day remain buried here. Winter is considered a time for the people of the doomed encampment to sleep.

Self-guided snowshoe and ski tours access the historic sites. Visitors should arrive during daylight, get an interpretive trail guide, and plan four hours to ski and view indoor exhibits. Ranger-led programs tour the battle-field (skis only) several times during the winter. Call for schedules.

Three trails reveal different battle scenes. The 3-mile round-trip Nez Perce Camp Trail leads to the former Indian camp. From the Visitor Center, ski south on the groomed route .25 mile. The trail then turns northwest for .5 mile, then east at the sign of the camp for the final .75 mile. Here the soldiers attacked the Nez Perce as they slept, firing point blank into tipis. Tipi poles stand in the meadow.

The trail passes a variety of habitats near the North Fork of the Big Hole River, including meadows, sagebrush benchland, and willow riparian areas. Across the river and to the northwest rises the 7,325-foot Battle Mountain, where the Nez Perce grazed their horses on the treeless, grassy slopes known as the Horse Pasture. Beyond rises the Anaconda

Directions at a glance

Park at the trailhead, a small pull-off on the left side as you enter the Big Hole National Battlefield. The Visitor Center is ahead .3 mile. The trail begins on a snow covered road so there is a gate across the front of the trail. The trail heads west from the pull-off.

Pintlar Wilderness, including Saddle Mountain's twin peaks, West Goat Peak at 10,793 feet and East Goat Peak at 10,399 feet.

From the Visitor Center, the 2-mile round-trip Siege Area Trail begins on the Camp Trail. After .75 mile on the Camp Trail, the Siege Area Trail heads north across a bridge to the site of the defensive position taken by the retreating soldiers. After the early morning surprise attack on the sleeping Nez Perce encampment failed, warriors rallied, forcing the soldiers to retreat up Battle Gulch Draw. The soldiers dug rifle pits and were held by the Nez Perce warriors for the remainder of the battle, providing time for the Nez Perce families to escape. Stay to the right/northwest at each place the trail splits. The trail leads to the Siege Area and the monument for the soldiers and volunteers who died here. To the left/west on the edge of the forest and before entering into the Siege Area, skiers will find the Howitzer Capture site, where the Nez Perce captured the army's sole howitzer and its reserve rifle ammunition, about .3 mile uphill. The ungroomed trail is steep. Skiers can skirt the edge of the trees to reach the capture site. There are spectacular views of the valley, the Big Hole Mountains, and 8,205-foot Ruby Peak.

The 6-mile round-trip Nez Perce National Historic Trail departs from the Siege Trail. After the first trail junction with the Nez Perce Camp Trail, continue north on the Siege Trail for about 300 meters to the trail junction sign. Turn left/west and ski 3 miles on an ungroomed Forest Service trail. The trail dead ends at the highway. Skiers may have to do some "fence-hopping" on this historic route of the Lewis and Clark Expedition. There are views of the Big Hole Valley, Ruby Peak, and the Pintlars. Some open steeps invite telemark turns.

How to get there

From Wisdom, drive west on Highway 43 for 15 miles to the Big Hole National Battlefield turnoff. If driving from Lost Trail Pass on Highway 93, turn east on Highway 43 and drive east 17 miles. At mile marker 16.5, turn north on the road into the battlefield and park in the plowed area. The center is clearly visible from the highway.

Discovery Basin and Georgetown Lake Trails

Anaconda, Montana

Type of trail:	▬ ⬤ ◀
Also used by:	Snowmobilers on some trails
Distance:	24 miles/40 kilometers
Terrain:	Rolling hills to mountainous
Trail difficulty:	Easy to more difficult
Surface quality:	4 kilometers of groomed skate and 36 kilometers of skier-groomed classic
Elevation:	6,400 to 7,103 feet
Food and facilities:	Sven's Bicycles of Anaconda rents ski equipment and ice skates, and can provide maps and advice for trails and backcountry routes. Discovery Basin Ski Area's day lodge, located at the trailhead, provides food services, ski and snowshoe rentals, and ski lessons. Butte's Pipestone Mountaineering has snowshoes and cross-country and backcountry skis. Georgetown lodging includes the Seven Gables Resort, Georgetown Lake Lodge, and the Pintlar Inn. Anaconda lodging includes the Hickory Street Inn, the Trade Wind Motel, and the Marcus Daly Motel. Fairmont Hot Springs Resort, 25 miles from the trailhead, is a full-service resort with two Olympic-size pools, two soaking pools, and a 350-foot waterslide with natural hot-springs water. Anaconda restaurants include Donivans' and Granny's.
Phone numbers:	Sven's Bicycles of Anaconda (406) 563–7988. Discovery Basin Ski Area (406) 563–2184. Pipestone Mountaineering (406) 782–4994. Seven Gables Resort (406) 563–5052. Georgetown Lake Lodge (406) 563–7020. Pintlar Inn (406) 563–5072. Hickory House Inn (406) 563–5481. Trade Wind Motel (800) 231–2660. Marcus Daly Motel (800) 535–6528. Fairmont Hot Springs Resort (800) 332–3272. Deerlodge National Forest (406) 859–3211. Emergency 911 alerts the sheriff's office. Cell phones work sporadically.

High in the Anaconda Mountain Range of western Montana, skiers find a remote set of backcountry trails popular for the cold snow, sheltered terrain, and unique history. The area was first developed through silver and copper mining operations, thus the name of the nearby alpine ski area, Discovery Basin. The area was once the focus of a corrupt political battle between frontier towns vying to become Montana's state cap-

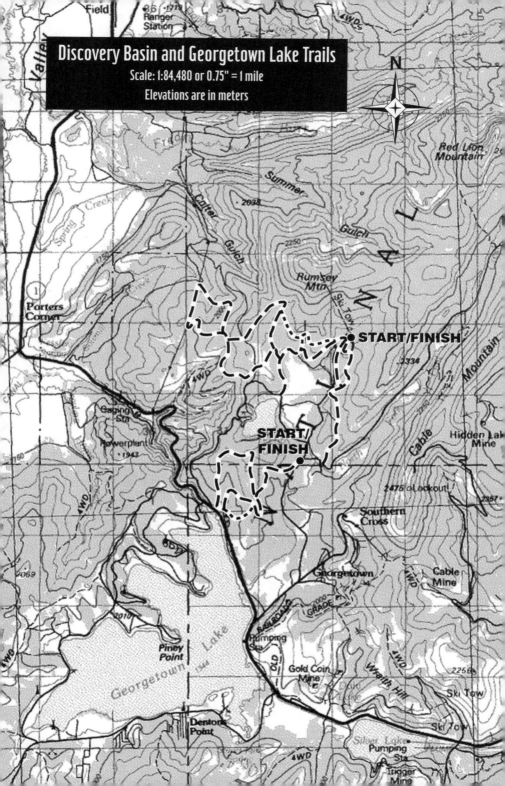

ital. Millionaire Marcus Daly pushed for his company town, Anaconda, at the foot of the mountains, while rival William Andrews Clark fought for Helena. Free drinks, cigars, and dollars flowed to voters and resulted in the 1894 decision for Helena. Anaconda's landmark copper smelter and tailings became a Superfund cleanup site and today is capped by a golf course designed by Jack Nicklaus.

Several trails depart from the base of Discovery Basin Ski Area. Trails primarily follow old logging roads and begin at 6,850 feet elevation with a groomed loop where skate skiers do daily laps. Beginners find the gentle terrain, cold snow, and grooming suitable for learning. The Discovery, Echo Lake, Cabin, Jack Pine, Powerline, and Rumsey trails all depart the parking area heading west on Discovery loop. The easiest route, Discovery, has a suggested counterclockwise direction. The trail has only about a 50-foot elevation change.

Beyond the groomed route, the Cabin Cutoff Trail and the Cabin Trail leave Discovery at the overhead powerline, turning right/west onto an ungroomed, more difficult trail. These trails are named for a broken-down trapper's or prospector's cabin at trailside, although locals say that if skiers head 10 feet in any direction, they'll find a dilapidated cabin. The Cabin Trail is a rudimentary and sometimes narrow trail with only a few trail markers stapled to trees. New snow makes route-finding difficult.

A suggested alternative is the easier Echo Lake from Discovery Trail. Ski Discovery about 1 kilometer, twice passing the Cabin Cutoff Trail and the Cabin Trail, and follow the sign to Echo Lake. The final few kilometers descend about 140 feet to Echo Lake. The return trip is on the same route to the Powerline Trail, turning right/southeast and skiing Powerline to the next junction, and then turning right/east for 1 kilometer to the trailhead. A snowmobile club maintains trails near the lake. Quiet weekdays offer excellent skate-skiing on the snowmobile trails.

A most challenging and lengthy 11-kilometer ski includes both the Jack Pine Trail and the Rumsey Trail. Although the trail map shows that you can ski from the Cabin Trail to Jack Pine, the better choice is to ski the Discovery Trail toward Echo Lake to the Jack Pine and Rumsey Trails. Look for the wooden trail sign and turn right/north. The Rumsey Trail incorporates both old road and single-track. It can be challenging, especially if it has been skied and then frozen. There are views of the Flint Creek Range, Flint Creek Valley, the Pintlar Range, and Evan's Peak.

The Cable Loop Trail and the Cable Campground Trail begin at the first, southeastern parking lot. Cable Loop heads south for 1.5 kilometers, where the trail meets the Cable Campground Trail. Cable Campground Trail is another old logging road with single-track sections. Skiers can either return to the parking area on the Cable Loop or turn south

onto the Cable Campground Trail and ski south 1.4 miles to the campground. Cable Loop is skier-tracked and generally downhill to 6,646 feet elevation. The return trip climbs among lodgepoles back to Discovery's parking area.

Lodgepole Ridge Trail has a separate trailhead. Check at Sven's Bicycles of Anaconda for directions and ski conditions for this 7.7-kilometer route.

How to get there

From Anaconda, drive to Georgetown Lake, 17 miles northwest on Highway 1. From Philipsburg, drive Highway 1 south 10 miles to Georgetown Lake. Turn east on Discovery Basin Road at Seven Gables and follow signs to Discovery Basin Ski Area, 5 miles.

Directions at a glance

To reach the trailhead for the Echo Lake Trail, Lost Trail, and Rumsey Trail, park in the parking lot farthest to the left/west and look for the small sign with the cross-country skier symbol. Trails head west. For the Cable Loop Trail and Cable Campground Trail, park in the southeastern parking area. Trails head south.

Mt. Haggin Nordic Ski Area
Anaconda, Montana

Type of trail: ▬▬ ◀

Also used by: Backcountry skiers

Distance: 15 miles/25 kilometers

Terrain: Meadows to rolling hills and a few steep climbs

Trail difficulty: Easy to most difficult

Surface quality: Machine-groomed

Elevation: 6,600 to 7,400 feet

Food and facilities: The Mile High Nordic Ski Club maintains the trails and the warming hut at the trailhead. There are no outhouses available. Skis are available in Anaconda at Sven's Bicycles and in Butte at Pipestone Mountaineering. Anaconda's restaurants include Barkley's, Donivans', and Granny's. Butte restaurants include the Uptown Cafe, Spaghettini for pasta, Lamplighter for prime rib, Acoma Restaurant, and Ipity Bop for pizza. Lodging choices include the Hickory House Inn in Anaconda, and the Copper King Mansion, the Best Western, and many others in Butte. Fairmont Hot Springs Resort is in nearby Gregson.

Phone numbers: Mile High Ski Club (406) 782–0316 or (406) 494–4235. Sven's Bicycles (406) 563–7988. Pipestone Mountaineering (406) 782–4994. Anaconda Chamber of Commerce (406) 563–2400. Butte Chamber of Commerce (800) 735–6814. Hickory House Inn (406) 563–5481. Copper King Mansion (406) 782–7580. Best Western (800) 543–5814. Fairmont Hot Springs Resort (800) 332–3272. Emergency 911 alerts the sheriff's office. Avalanche advisory (406) 587–6981.

The Butte-Anaconda area dishes up glittering histories of the riches, fame—and disasters—of the great mining boom of a century ago. There are remnants of the mining era across the landscape and communities of south-central Montana. In Butte, "the richest hill on earth," visitors can stay in the century-old Copper King Mansion, a veritable monument to the riches unearthed here. In the late 1800s, Butte led the country in metal mining and influenced the world economy.

The Mt. Haggin Nordic ski trails meander through the state-owned Mt. Haggin Wildlife Management Area, home to moose, coyotes, snowshoe hares, and great horned owls. Most trails are groomed for classic skiing. Two trails, Crooked John Loop and Sugarloaf Loop, are also groomed for skate skiing. The Spire Loop remains ungroomed.

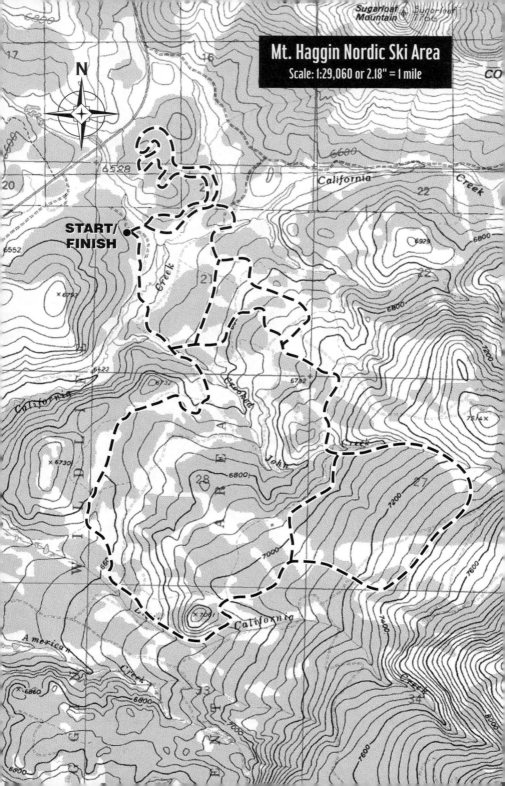

From the warming hut, beginners ski lower Crooked John Loop. Crooked John begins heading south from the hut, offering some moderate hills on the 5-kilometer trail. The sparse trees, mostly lodgepole pines, allow for views toward the Continental Divide to the east. At the first junction, 1.1 kilometers from the trailhead, Crooked John turns left/east. The next junction, about .1 kilometer later, heads north and makes a shortcut through the middle of Crooked John, eliminating 1.7 kilometers of the loop. It joins the trail again after .5 kilometer. Notice the landmark, the 7,766-foot pointed peak called Sugarloaf Mountain, northeast of the trailhead. Take the left/north route and follow the trail back to the warming hut.

From the first Crooked John Loop, skiers access the longest routes of the Little California Loop and Spire Loop, both of which offer outstanding panoramic views of the 10,000-foot Pintlar Range to the west. At 1.1 kilometers and the first junction, continue south onto Little California Loop, groomed for classic skiing. The 10.8-kilometer total from the hut and back is dominated by hill climbing, then rewarded at the end by cruising downhills. About 3.5 kilometers from the Crooked John intersection, the Little California Loop climbs alongside Little California Creek for about .75 kilometer. The trail eventually climbs past some old cabins and to 7,100 feet, where it meets the Spire Loop Trail. Take the left/north route to stay on Little California and cruise 1 kilometer before the downhills begin. An especially exciting schuss is the Sleepy Hollow 1.2-kilometer cutoff back to Crooked John Loop and the trailhead.

The Spire Loop Trail is well worth the added 2.9 kilometers. This ungroomed route climbs steeply from 7,100 feet to 7,400 in a mere .5 kilometer. Rewards include awesome views of the high mountain plateau, the Pintlars, and magnificent spires just off the trail. Once at 7,400 feet, the trail cruises northeast below the crags. Telemarkers access the Continental Divide by climbing east past the spires (skins and edged skis are necessary) to 7,800 feet or higher in a .5-kilometer climb. Views from the top of the Divide include the Big Hole Valley and Butte. Some skiers climb over the Divide and ski down to Fairmont Hot Springs, about a 14-mile trip requiring a shuttle vehicle, backcountry equipment, and telemarking skills in the cold powder snow. Spire Loop Trail turns west and descends to 7,000 feet and the next junction with Little California. Turn right/north and ski about 3 kilometers back to the warming hut.

Skiers from the Mike High Nordic Ski Club "howl with the wolf" on full-moon nights. The officially unorganized full-moon ski trips on January, February, and March nights often see below-zero temperatures. Skiers should carry headlamps.

How to get there

From Butte drive west on Interstate 90 for 20 miles and take the Anaconda exit, Exit 208, onto Highway 1. As you cross the railroad tracks, look for the sign to Wisdom. Turn left and drive 11 miles south on Highway 274. Turn left/east into the parking area.

Alice Creek Ranch
Lincoln, Montana

Type of trail:	▬ ◉ ◄
Also used by:	Telemarkers; also snowmobilers outside the ranch property
Distance:	24 miles/40 kilometers
Terrain:	Flat meadows, hilly forests, and telemark hills
Trail difficulty:	Easiest to most difficult
Surface quality:	Machine-groomed daily for classic and skate lane; separate snowshoe trails; backcountry access available.
Elevation:	5,400 to 6,800 feet
Food and facilities:	Alice Creek Ranch offers a full-service lodge, open Thursdays through Sundays, and two backcountry cabin rentals. Cabin guests cook their own grits on a wood cookstove. Snacks, hot chocolate, and trail passes can be purchased at the trailhead yurt. There is an outhouse at the trailhead and another outhouse on the S Loop at the South Fork Cabin. Ski lessons and equipment rentals are available by reservation. Lincoln has some services but no ski shops. The nearest ski shops are in Helena and Great Falls. Locals suggest the 7-Up Ranch Supper Club or the Stone Wall Steak House in Lincoln for dinner.
Phone numbers:	Alice Creek Ranch (406) 362–4865. Lincoln Ranger District, Helena National Forest (406) 362–4265. 7-Up Ranch Supper Club (406) 362–4255. Lincoln Valley Chamber of Commerce (406) 362–4949. Emergency 911 alerts the sheriff's office. Cell phones generally do not work here. Avalanche forecast (800) 281–1030 or (406) 549–4488.

Salish, Kootenai, and Blackfeet Indians were the original travelers through the mountains surrounding the ranch, en route to the bison herds of the plains. The Lewis and Clark Corps of Discovery crossed what is now Alice Creek ranchland, according to the U.S. Forest Service. The nearest town, Lincoln, sprouted from the dust—gold dust, that is—in 1865, with the discovery of gold in nearby streams. Mines still operate in the area. Lincoln's most notorious resident, "Unabomber" Ted Kaczynski, was arrested in April 1996 and later convicted of bombings that killed three and injured twenty-three people. The rest of the local population is pretty darn friendly.

Alice Creek Ranch is a working cattle operation and guest ranch high in the Rocky Mountains. The superbly groomed trails roll along some of the 3,000 ranch acres at the edge of the Scapegoat Wilderness. By sum-

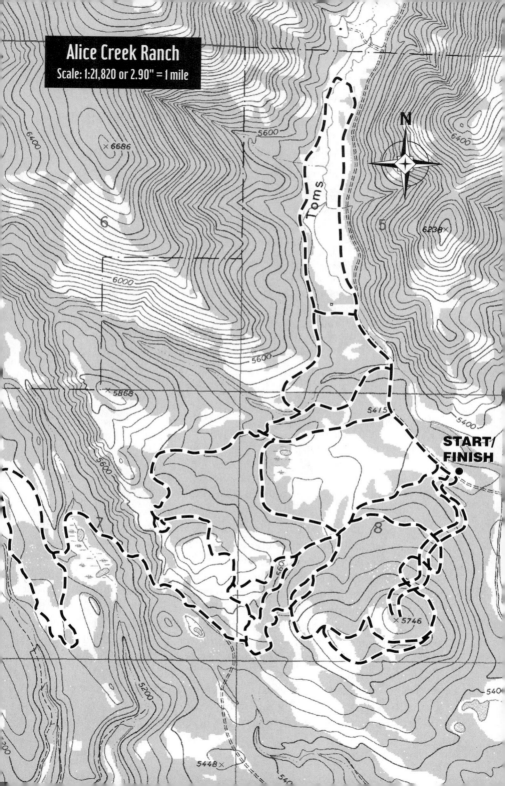

mer, 600 Hereford cattle roam the ranch as they have for the past seventy summers.

Day skiers and snowshoers find well-groomed and well-marked skier-only trails. Snowmobiles are not allowed on any ranch property. Skate skiers find high-quality routes that challenge racers-in-training. From the yurt, skiers head west on the Meadow Loop, a gentle, rolling 3-kilometer ski around a natural meadow area. Several options provide for longer distances off this counterclockwise loop. From the first junction at 1 kilometer, skiers can access Tom's Gulch Trail, a 3-kilometer loop that follows Tom's Creek and provides views of Silver King Mountain at 6,612 feet and Red Mountain at over 8,000 feet.

Overnight guests choose between the homey guest lodge, located at ranch headquarters, and backcountry cabins lit only by starlight and a few propane lanterns. To access the South Fork Cabin, skiers start on the Meadow Loop and ski to Junction 3, then turn left onto the South Fork Trail. Ski 1.5 kilometers to the cabin. From the trailhead, the overall climb of 200 feet is over varied terrain among aspen and evergreen trees. The trail squeaks through the middle of a homestead area, which includes two cabins, an outhouse, and other outbuildings. The view into the Scapegoat Wilderness includes Silver King Mountain at 6,612 feet.

Snowshoers have a 5-kilometer route to themselves. The groomed snowshoe trail departs from the yurt heading southeast on the Snowshoe Trail. It travels south of the K2 Ski Trail and nears the South Fork Cabin. Snowshoers have access to much of the ranch by making their own trails.

Snowcat tours climb to the top of either the K2 Ski Trail or Bubba's Hill north of the yurt to bowl-skiing terrain for telemarkers. Rates are $300 per day; minimum two, maximum seven skiers.

How to get there

From Missoula, drive 85 miles east on U.S. Highway 200 to Alice Creek Road. From Lincoln, drive 8 miles east on U.S. Highway 200. From Great Falls, drive 68 miles west on U.S. Highway 200. A quarter mile east of the Bouma Post Yard (fence post manufacturing), turn north on Alice Creek Road. Drive 5 miles north on this well-maintained, gravel road to the ranch.

Lewis and Clark Pass/Rogers Pass
Lincoln, Montana

Type of trail: ▬▬ ⬤

Also used by: Alpine touring skiers

Distance: 160 miles/256 kilometers

Terrain: Mountainous

Trail difficulty: Most difficult to extreme

Surface quality: Variable backcountry; use edged skis and climbing skins

Elevation: 5,400 to 8,500 feet

Food and facilities: The closest town is Lincoln, 10 miles west; the state capital, Helena, is 50 miles east. Alice Creek Ranch offers the nearest lodging to the trailheads. Helena has several good restaurants, such as the Windbag, Ryan and Maclean's Tea Room, and Toi's Thai, as well as major hotel chains. Dining in Lincoln includes the 7-Up Supper Club. Ski equipment is available in Helena at The Base Camp and at Bob Ward & Sons.

Phone numbers: Lincoln Ranger District (406) 362–4265. Helena Ranger District (406) 449–5490. Alice Creek Ranch (406) 362–4865. The 7-Up Ranch Supper Club (406) 362–4255. Lincoln Valley Chamber of Commerce (406) 362–4949. The Base Camp (406) 443–5360. Bob Ward & Sons (406) 443–2138. Helena Chamber of Commerce (406) 442–4120. Emergency 911 alerts the sheriff's office. Cell phones generally do not work here. Avalanche forecast (800) 281–1030 or (406) 549–4488.

The Continental Divide runs north-south through Montana, slicing the state into distinct west and east sides and very different weather patterns. During the winter the Continental Divide Trail can be accessed at only a few mountain passes. Parts of the trail are skiable, although it varies from challenging, day-tripper's backcountry to extreme expedition skiing. A major portion of the trail, more than 100 miles between Rogers Pass and Marias Pass, is not crossed by roads.

The routes from the Lewis and Clark Pass north to the Scapegoat Wilderness and down to the trailhead, or alternatively from Lewis and Clark Pass south to Roger's Pass, both offer moderate climbs and outstanding vistas. These routes should include an overnight camp. Access is via the Nordic trailhead at Alice Creek Ranch near Lincoln. Permission is necessary to park at the ranch's parking area. Another option is arranging to be dropped off at the ranch.

Ski 5 miles north of Alice Creek Ranch on the unplowed portion of

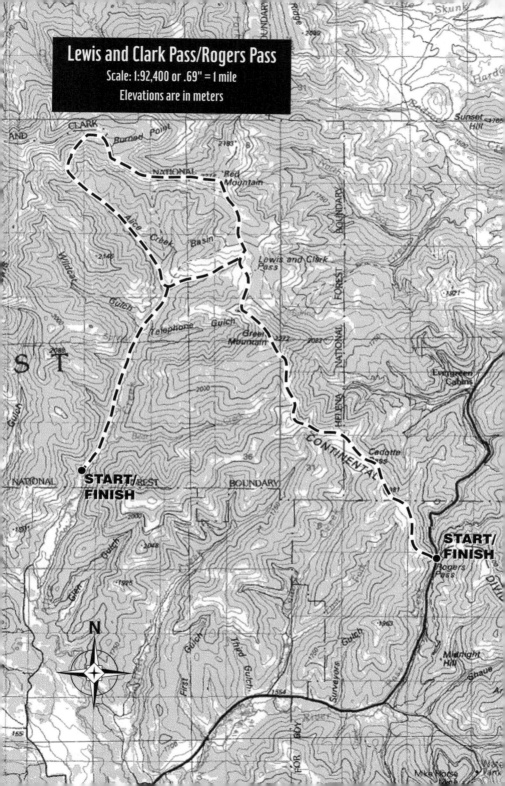

Lewis and Clark Pass/Rogers Pass
Scale: 1:92,400 or .69" = 1 mile
Elevations are in meters

START/FINISH

START/FINISH
Rogers Pass

N

Alice Creek Road. The unmarked trailhead is obvious because the road ends at a gate and horse-hitch rails. Note that some maps show a nonexistent ranger station at road's end. Winter campers might choose the basin area to camp. The unmarked Forest Service trail (a closed jeep trail) follows the East Fork of Alice Creek, climbing from 5,500 to 6,421 feet in 1.5 miles on a road grade. Once over the gate, ski northeast on the creek's north edge. The final .5 mile includes two moderate switchbacks up to Lewis and Clark Pass on the Continental Divide. There should be a sign at the summit just after you go through an open gate. Vandals sometimes destroy the sign; if no sign is visible, the summit is obvious with unobstructed views east and west. The Lewis and Clark Expedition crossed the mountains here in July 1806.

A 16-mile loop that includes Lewis and Clark Pass takes skiers north into a proposed extension of the Scapegoat Wilderness. After skiing 6.5 miles to Lewis and Clark Pass, travel north on the Continental Divide Trail. The trail junction with Trail #440 is 3 miles north of the pass. At the junction, turn west on Trail #440 and travel down 3 miles to the horse-hitch rails. There is some avalanche danger near the top of the telemark terrain in this area. Return 5 miles south on Alice Creek Road to the ranch.

A 12.5-mile route heads south from Lewis and Clark Pass and requires a vehicle shuttle. From Lewis and Clark Pass, the 6 miles along the spine of the continent to 6,376-foot Rogers Pass includes views east to the Helena Valley. Challenging elevation changes dominate the route and include three mountains to ascend and descend. The trail passes Green Mountain on the east and an area frequented by eagles during their fall and spring migration. Depending on wind and weather, there may be exposed grassy or bald, rocky spots close to Rogers Pass. Rogers Pass is named for a railroad surveyor but is most famous as the coldest recorded spot in the nation. On January 20, 1954, the National Weather Service recorded the temperature at minus 69.7 degrees F. Check locally for snow conditions; during some winters the strong winds prevent snow from accumulating on this route.

The ultimate backcountry trip on the Continental Divide Trail begins at Rogers Pass and heads 161 miles north to Marias Pass through the Scapegoat and Bob Marshall Wilderness areas. Skiers completing the 10-day expedition report that the trail offers challenging ridge-line cruising, serious windblown crust, and hike-only bare ground swept clean by the wind. Extreme exposure points force skiers to remove skis, strap them to packs, and crawl across knife-edges with cliffs on both sides.

How to get there

Drive to Alice Creek Ranch, 8 miles east of Lincoln on Highway 200. From Great Falls, drive 68 miles west on U.S. Highway 200 to Alice Creek Road. Turn north on Alice Creek Road and drive 5 miles to the ranch and the end of the plowing.

Rogers Pass is 15 miles east of Lincoln on Highway 200 and 60 miles west of Helena on Highway 200. If it's snowing heavily, do not park here. Wait until an area is plowed out on either side of highway.

Directions at a glance

Turn left/west into the ranch parking lot off Alice Creek Road and park near the yurt. Get permission to leave a vehicle before heading into the backcountry. At Rogers Pass, park at the plowed areas along the highway. Look for the trail sign; if it is buried in snow, climb the north bank and ski the ridge line north.

Stemple Pass
Lincoln, Montana

Type of trail:	▬▬
Also used by:	Wildlife
Distance:	14 miles/22.4 kilometers
Terrain:	Gentle grades to steeper routes with sharp turns
Trail difficulty:	Easiest to more difficult
Surface quality:	Skier-packed
Elevation:	6,376 to 6,750 feet
Food and facilities:	Outhouses at the trailhead are next to the large trail sign near the middle of the parking area. There are no other facilities. Most skiers access Stemple from Helena or Great Falls, where a number of good eateries and lodging facilities can be found. Helena has several good restaurants, such as the Windbag, Ryan and Maclean's Tea Room, and Toi's Thai. Helena and Great Falls have several major hotel chains. Ski equipment is available in Helena at The Base Camp and at Bob Ward & Sons.
Phone numbers:	The nearest public telephones are in Lincoln and Canyon Creek. Helena National Forest (406) 362–4265. The Base Camp (406) 443–5360. Bob Ward & Sons (406) 443–2138. Helena Chamber of Commerce (406) 442–4120. Skiers needing assistance can call (406) 447–8293, or in case of emergency, 911 alerts the Lewis and Clark County Sheriff's office.

Stemple Pass skiers consider this area their own private playground and hope that it remains a primitive experience, which means trails are skier-packed. There are some popular off-piste routes for telemarking or bushwhacking. Most skiers stick to the four ski loops. The pass sits at 6,376 feet on the southern rim of the Blackfoot Valley. Here the snow blows in deep from early December until late March, and can reach depths of up to 5 feet. Stemple Pass was once a toll road between Helena and Lincoln during the gold-mining boomtown days of Lincoln in the 1860s. No tolls are collected for skiing Stemple Pass. Stemple crosses the Continental Divide in Montana. The notorious "Unabomber" lived at the pass's western foot for twenty years.

Visitors must remember that weather can brew some wicked storms over the Continental Divide. They should be prepared for quickly changing weather and be on the lookout for wildlife. The Forest Service's infor-

Stemple Pass

Scale: 1:16,000 or 3.96" = 1 mile

mation at the trailhead reminds visitors that the animals have a difficult time surviving in winter and people should never approach any wildlife. Undue strain or exertion from running may cause death to animals. Skiers should make a wide detour around moose, deer, or elk on the trail.

Ski north on the marked ski trails. All trails begin from the easy, 1.25-mile North Stemple Loop. This gentle and wide grade allows beginners the opportunity for an out-and-back ski while experiencing the wilds of the backcountry. There is only a 35-foot elevation gain over the North Stemple Loop.

The North Meadow Loop, an intermediate route that follows the Continental Divide, begins at the marked trail junction and to the left/west off North Stemple. Most skiers take North Meadow in a clockwise direction. After a tenth of a mile, the North Meadow splits. Stay to the left. Ski north for 1.25 miles, at which point you can either loop back on North Meadow or take the .75-mile Crossover Loop for the longest ski on the trails. Skiers can access Divide Loop from North Meadow's eastern loop.

Divide Loop is the most challenging of the trails and connects North Meadow with North Stemple. At the highest point of the North Meadow Loop, the easternmost section of the route, turn northeast and follow the

Continental Divide National Scenic Trail. After 100 meters, views open up to the east and north as the trail enters a partially regrown clearcut. Fifty meters into the clearcut, at a trail junction, the remainder of the Divide Loop heads sharply right/east and descends steeply to North Stemple, finally heading south back to the parking area. If you turn north at the junction, the trail descends steeply for .25 mile through a series of curves to the northern end of marked trails. Ambitious skiers can continue northeast off the trail system and onto the sparsely-signed Continental Divide National Scenic Trail for 1.5 miles. Descend through a meadow into the beautiful Rooster Bill drainage to the south. A marked trail heads 3 miles down the drainage to the plowed road on the east side of Stemple Pass. Leave a shuttle at the Rooster Bill Creek crossing on Stemple Pass Road, but ask permission at the cabin to ski through the cabin owner's property. The 5.5-mile ski includes views of surrounding peaks, good telemark turning, and a trail through old-growth forest.

How To Get There

The road to Stemple Pass is a well-maintained "mail route" that is plowed to perfection. Even so, it is narrow, winding, and sometimes icy. From Helena, take Interstate 15 north 6 miles to the Lincoln Road exit. After exiting, drive northwest on Lincoln Road 32 miles. Turn left/west on Stemple Pass Road and drive 6 miles to the pass.

MacDonald Pass
Helena, Montana

Type of trail: ▬▬ ⬭ ⟨

Also used by: Wildlife

Distance: 10.2 miles/17 kilometers

Terrain: Gentle hills to hilly

Trail difficulty: Easy to moderate

Surface quality: Machine-groomed intermittently

Elevation: 5,900 to 6,200 feet

Food and facilities: All services are available in nearby Helena, 12 miles east of the pass. The Base Camp and Bob Ward & Sons in Helena rent and sell ski equipment. There is a pit toilet 50 meters down the trail from the parking area. Frontier Town, not far from the trailhead, serves food. In Helena, good restaurants include The Windbag and Salvatore's. Helena has its share of major hotel chains and restaurants.

Phone numbers: Helena Ranger District (406) 449–5490. Lincoln Ranger District (406) 362–4265. The Base Camp (406) 443–5360. Bob Ward & Sons (406) 443–2138. Helena Chamber of Commerce (406) 442–4120. Emergency 911. Cell phones offer limited service in the mountains.

MacDonald Pass is one of a few places where a major winter road crosses the Continental Divide, offering easy access to ski trails. The Forest Service maintains a trail system just east of the pass in a sheltered forest area that is actually below the Continental Divide itself. Yet views east to the Big Belt Mountains are no less stunning from the four loop trails than from the divide itself. The valley below holds Helena, Montana's state capital, famous for its main street, Last Chance Gulch. Much of this area boomed during the gold rush that began in 1864. There is very little mining in the area today; the major industries are tourism and government services. Helena was named the seat of the territorial government in 1875 and became the state capital when Montana was granted statehood in 1889.

MacDonald Pass trails are groomed as needed by the Last Chance Nordic Ski Club. All four trails begin on the easiest Old Cabin Loop Trail, a 2.8-mile ski trip. Maps at the trailhead indicate which direction to ski on the loops. After leaving the parking area and passing the trailhead sign, there is an initial steep section that can be icy. Beginners might consider walking down the first hill and putting on their skis at the bottom.

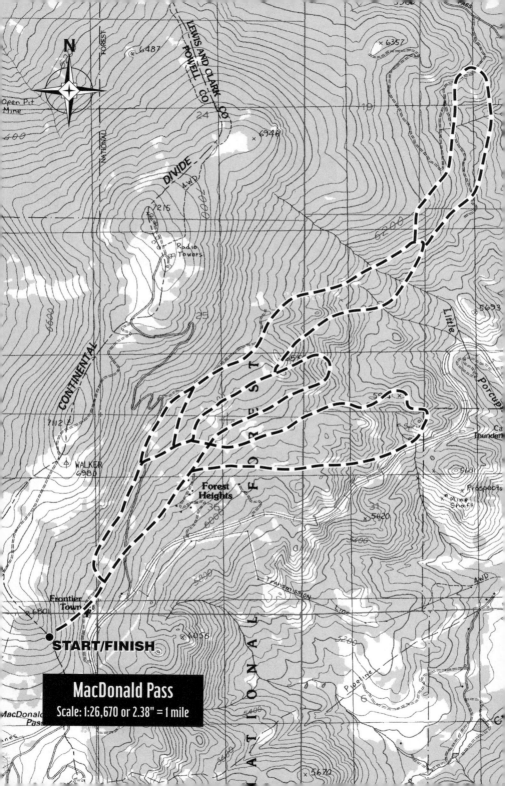

MacDonald Pass
Scale: 1:26,670 or 2.38" = 1 mile

START/FINISH

Frontier Town

Forest Heights

WALKER 6980

CONTINENTAL DIVIDE

4WD

Radio Towers

LEWIS AND CLARK CO.
POWELL CO.

FOREST

NATIONAL

Open Pit Mine

6487

6948

7215

6357

5653

Little Porcupine

Thunder

Prospects

Mine Shaft

5620

6056

5890

Pipeline

5670

MacDonald Pass

NATIONAL

The ski patrol cabin, trail maps, and a pit toilet are at trailside just a short distance along the trail. Continue north at all trail intersections to remain on the Old Cabin Loop Trail. There is a picnic spot at 1.4 miles. A three-sided shelter with a barbecue grill is available for public use. Skiers pack charcoal and picnic supplies to the shelter, which is especially popular on weekends. The trail loops around the shelter for the return trip. Maintain a southerly route on the way back.

The first intersection off the Old Cabin Loop at .75 mile is the end of Meadows Loop. To ski Meadows, continue north to the second right/east turn for the 3.6-mile round trip. Meadows is considered most difficult because of steep pitches and sharp turns at the bottom of hills.

The longest trail begins .1 mile past the Old Cabin Loop shelter, with a sharp right/north turn onto Big Pine Loop. After .75 mile, Big Pine turns back south, but skiers can access Little Porcupine Loop for a total round trip of 6 miles. Both Big Pine and Little Porcupine are considered more difficult routes mainly due to their length.

Snowshoers and classic tourists like the 4-mile climb toward Priest Pass, turning around at the microwave tower. Telemarkers tackle moderate slopes and drifts here. After the microwave tower, the Continental Divide Trail intersects, and there is considerable route finding to get to Priest Pass. Round trip would be 14 miles on trail that is challenging because of the distance and elevation gain. The trail is a one-lane road called the Microwave Road, which may be marked by the tracks of snow-machines en route to service the microwave towers. Some adventurers park at MacDonald Pass, ski past the microwave towers north to Priest Pass, and turn east down the snowed-in Priest Pass Road for a 12-mile challenging ski. A shuttle vehicle would need to be parked at the eastern foot of MacDonald Pass.

How to get there

From Helena, drive 12 miles west on Highway 12 toward MacDonald Pass. Look for the large sign on the right/north side of the road for Frontier Town and turn right/north on Frontier Town Road. Park by the large buffalo statue but not on the road.

Kings Hill Pass
Neihart, Montana

Type of trail:	▬▬ ⬭
Also used by:	Telemarkers, snowmobiles
Distance:	17 miles/27.2 kilometers
Terrain:	Meadows, gentle slopes, hills, and mountains
Trail difficulty:	Moderate to most difficult
Surface quality:	Skier-packed
Elevation:	5,600 to 7,393 feet
Food and facilities:	The closest restaurant, bar, and cross-country ski rentals are available at Showdown Ski Area on Kings Hill Pass. The small communities of White Sulphur Springs, Neihart, and Monarch have most services. Great Falls, 70 miles northwest, has all services. Ski and snowshoe equipment is available at Showdown Ski Area. Equipment is also available in Great Falls at Big Horn Wilderness and at Big Bear Sports. Montana Mountain Lodge has homey lodging and full breakfast and dinner available about ten minutes from trailheads. Ask about the pomegranate sorbet! Historic lodging in Great Falls includes the Collins Mansion Bed and Breakfast and the Charlie Russell Manor Historic Bed and Breakfast. Try the Connection Supper Club or the Newland Creek Club for steaks in White Sulphur Springs. The chicken is good at the Mint Bar. The Belt Creek Brew Pub is located in the historic Pioneer Garage in Belt, 20 miles east of Great Falls on Highway 87/89.
Phone numbers:	Lewis and Clark National Forest/Kings Hill Ranger District (406) 547–3361. Showdown Ski Area (800) 433–0022. Big Horn Wilderness (406) 453–2841. Big Bear Sports (406) 721–6400. Montana Mountain Lodge (406) 547–3773. Collins Mansion Bed and Breakfast (877) 452–6798 or (406) 452–6798, 1003 2nd Avenue Northwest, Great Falls, MT, 59404. Charlie Russell Manor Historic Bed and Breakfast (406) 455–1400, 825 4th Avenue North, Great Falls, MT, 59401. Great Falls XC Ski Club, Box 2725, Great Falls, MT 59403. Emergency 911. Check with the ski patrol at Showdown Ski Area for avalanche conditions.

Two trails in the Little Belt Mountains lead skiers off the top of Kings Hill Pass beginning west and then either north or south and down different drainages for all-day trips. Both require a shuttle at trail's end. The

FINISH

START

FINISH

Kings Hill Pass
Scale: 1:112,740 or 0.56" = 1 mile
Elevations are in meters

N

region is known for the boom towns that grew up after the discovery of silver in the area during the 1880s. White Sulphur Springs was known to Native Americans as "medicine waters." The natural hot springs were developed first for miners to soak, then for a doctor's patients, and today attract guests for their supposed healing powers.

Kings Hill Pass is the highest pass that remains open in Montana in winter. The top, at 7,393 feet, receives the brunt of many cold winter storms. Because of the high elevation, Kings Hill receives cold, fine snow all winter. On clear days from the pass, it's possible to look south to the Castle Mountains and farther south down to Yellowstone National Park, into the Crazy Mountains, and west to the Big Belts. Over 200 miles of groomed snowmobile trails are nearby. The machines generally only cross ski trails or share the trails for short distances.

The O'Brien Creek Trail is a pleasant day trip and the easiest of the two trails. The backcountry touring has an overall elevation drop of about 1,700 feet north to Neihart. There may be creek crossings involved during the early or late season; skiers will need to find a log to cross.

The trail begins at the summit of Kings Hill Pass on the west side of Highway 89, heading west toward Showdown Ski Area. It starts as an old road from the Kings Hill Pass. Follow the edge of Porphyry Peak Road through a wooded area for less than a mile to the alpine ski area. The trail passes the Poma lift and climbs parallel to it. At the top ski north. After a mile in open terrain, the trail intersects Divide Road. Continue north following the O'Brien Creek drainage for the remainder of the trip. The trail passes O'Brien Park, a meadow area. Keep heading north. Be aware of an avalanche path 5 miles into the trail. Send one skier at a time if reports suggest that avalanche danger exists.

A similar route from Kings Hill Pass heads south on the Porphyry Peak/Ranch Creek Trail. This downhill trail also requires a shuttle or vehicle left on Highway 89 at Forest Green. This advanced trail is popular with backcountry telemarkers skiing down Porphyry Peak and maybe Mizpah Peak before the final descent on Ranch Creek Trail. It is avalanche-prone territory. Park a shuttle vehicle on Highway 89 at the Forest Green Restaurant.

The trail directions are the same for O'Brien Creek Trail to Showdown. After passing the Poma lift at Showdown Ski Area, climb Porphyry Peak Road to the summit ridge. Climbing skins are helpful, although many skiers purchase a lift pass to access the top of 8,192-foot Porphyry Peak. The trail turns south after 1.25 miles. After another mile, the trail passes the Mizpah Ridge Shelter. Mizpah Bowls are avalanche-prone so skiers should check conditions for avalanche hazard. The trail slips past Mizpah Peak's western slope. Telemarkers might find some steeps and powder here. The route follows Ranch Creek drainage down

to the settlement of Forest Green, an old homestead area with summer cabins and the Forest Green Restaurant.

How to get there

From Great Falls, drive southeast on Highway 89/87/200 east for 61 miles to the summit of Kings Hill Pass. Park on the west side of the highway in the plowed area. If there is no safe parking spot, go to the entrance of Showdown Ski Area and park in Showdown's lot.

Directions at a glance

From Kings Hill Pass, look for the wide jeep trail heading west. If starting from Showdown's parking area, walk to the ski lifts, and turn right/north by the Poma Lift for the O'Brien Trail. Leave a vehicle near Bob's Bar in Neihart for the O'Brien Trail shuttle. To ski the Porphyry Peak/Ranch Creek Trail, leave a shuttle vehicle at the Forest Green Restaurant on Highway 89 south of the pass.

Silver Crest Cross Country Ski Trails

Neihart, Montana

Type of trail: ▬ ◄

Also used by: Backcountry skiers

Distance: 10.8 miles/18 kilometers

Terrain: Meadows, gentle slopes, hills and mountains

Trail difficulty: Easiest to more difficult

Surface quality: Machine-groomed weekly

Elevation: 7,000 to 7,243 feet

Food and facilities: The parking area has outhouses and trail information. There are two shelters on the trail system. The closest restaurant, bar, and telemark ski rentals are available at Showdown Ski Area on Kings Hill Pass. The small communities of White Sulphur Springs, Neihart, and Monarch have most services. Great Falls, 70 miles north and west, has all services. Cross-country equipment is available in Great Falls at Bighorn Wilderness, Knicker Biker, and Big Bear Sports. Montana Mountain Lodge, about fifteen minutes from the trailhead, has homey lodging and full breakfast and dinner available. Lodging is also available in White Sulphur Springs, Neihart, Monarch, and Great Falls. Historic lodging in Great Falls includes the Collins Mansion Bed and Breakfast and the Charlie Russell Manor Historic Bed and Breakfast. Try the Connection Supper Club and the homey Newlan Creek Club for steaks in White Sulphur, or check out the chicken at the Mint Bar. The Belt Creek Brew Pub is located in the historic Pioneer Garage in Belt, 20 miles east of Great Falls on Highway 87/89.

Phone numbers: Lewis and Clark National Forest/Kings Hill Ranger District (406) 547–3361. Showdown Ski Area (800) 433–0022. Bighorn Wilderness (406) 453–2841. Knicker Biker (406) 494–2912. Big Bear Sports (406) 721–6400. Montana Mountain Lodge (406) 547–3773. Great Falls XC Club, Box 2725, Great Falls, MT 59403. Collins Mansion Bed and Breakfast (877) 452–6798 or (406) 452–6798, 1003 2nd Avenue Northwest, Great Falls, MT, 59404. Charlie Russell Manor Historic Bed and Breakfast (406) 455–1400, 825 4th Avenue North, Great Falls, MT, 59401. Emergency 911. For avalanche information check with Showdown Ski Area's ski patrol (406) 236–5522.

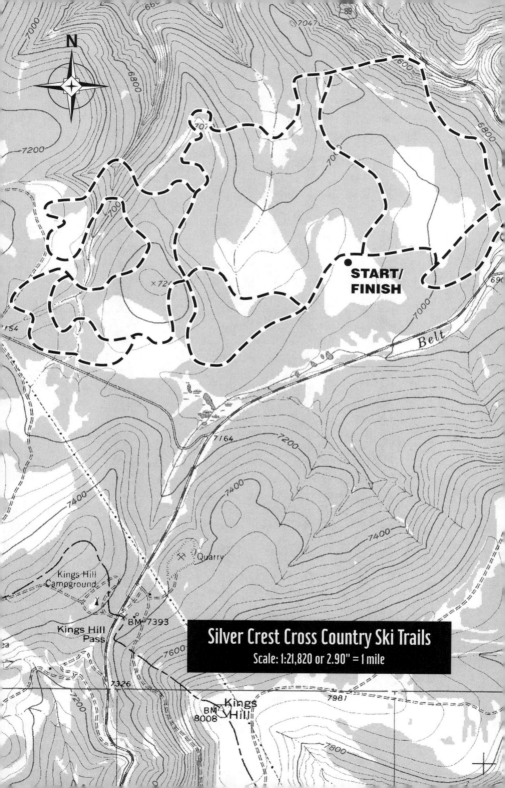

START/FINISH

Silver Crest Cross Country Ski Trails
Scale: 1:21,820 or 2.90" = 1 mile

N

Belt

Quarry

Kings Hill
Campground

Kings Hill
Pass

BM 7393

Kings
Hill

BM
8008

The Little Belt Mountains have yielded silver to miners for over a century. The Little Belts are also home to ranching, mining, and timber operations. Winter-sports enthusiasts find cold, dry snow at the 7,000-foot elevation. Nearby White Sulphur Springs attracts guests for the supposed healing powers of the hot springs.

Cross-country skiers find a bonanza in Charlie Russell County, where Russell painted his famous images of the wild West. Silver Crest Cross Country Ski Trails, on the Lewis and Clark National Forest near Neihart, are usually packed on Fridays and groomed on Saturdays by the Great Falls Cross Country Club. Note that the shared-use parking lot attracts snowmobilers, although there is a separate trail system with 200 miles of groomed snow-machine trails. The Silver Crest trails have 3.5 kilometers of easiest terrain, 10.3 kilometers considered more difficult, and 4.2 kilometers classified as most difficult. The Silver Crest trail system's four loops are set for classic and skate skiing but no snowshoes or dogs are allowed. The club sponsors an annual ski race, the Klister Klassic, in mid February for skiers of all ages and abilities. All loops begin at the shared-use parking area. Trails have suggested directions that are designated on signs and maps available at the trailhead and throughout the trail system. All trails are in the trees and protected from winds that can scour treeless areas.

An easy beginner loop starts from the parking area heading north on the B Loop. Ski east, counterclockwise, following 3.5-kilometer trail. Stay to the left at all intersections. About 1.8 kilometers from the trailhead is the 89er Overlook, with views into the canyon where the highway comes up from Neihart. You can also see Neihart and Baldy Peaks in the Little Belt Mountains. At the last intersection, the three-sided Silver Dyke Shelter invites skiers to take a break before skiing the final 1.1 kilometer.

From the Silver Dyke Shelter, skiers can opt to take another loop past Homestake Meadow, C Loop, for an additional 3.3-kilometer ski. This more challenging loop climbs some hills before dropping near the Sluice-box Run and returning on a gradual downhill to the trailhead. There are views of Porphyry Peak and Showdown Ski Area.

For a more challenging ski, take the outer loops, C to D to E, for a total 9-kilometer ski. Begin on B loop to the Silver Dyke Shelter. Turn right/west on C Loop at the junction by the shelter and remain on trails to the right for the full outer-loop ski. There are views of Piccea Creek, Porphyry Peak, and Showdown Ski Area. Trails are well signed at each intersection. At nearly the outermost point is the Mt. Eureka Shelter at 7,245 feet elevation. From there, the route is another 5 kilometers to the trailhead. Backcountry skiers might use the groomed trail system off E Loop to access the O'Brien Creek Backcountry Ski Trail.

How to get there

From Great Falls, drive southeast on Highway 89/87/200 southeast for 61 miles. Turn right/northwest at the skier and snowmobile signs for the Kings Hill Winter Recreation Area parking lot. The parking area is .25 miles off the highway.

Directions at a glance

Trails begin on the west side of the first parking lot loop. Sign the registration book at the trailhead and drop in a donation for trail maintenance.

Bohart Ranch and Bozeman Area Trails

Bozeman, Montana

Type of trail:	▬ ⬮ ◄
Also used by:	Wildlife
Distance:	15 miles/25 kilometers
Terrain:	Rolling hills
Trail difficulty:	Easy to moderately difficult
Surface quality:	Machine-groomed daily
Elevation:	6,100 to 6,600 feet
Food and facilities:	The trailhead area has a warming hut, ski rentals, ski lessons, snacks, and deluxe outhouses. Some lodging is available at the alpine ski area next door. All services are available in Bozeman, including historic bed-and-breakfast inns, chain hotels, and restaurants. The Silver Forest Inn is about 1 mile from Bohart Ranch. The elegant and historic 1927 Gallatin Gateway Inn, between Bozeman and Big Sky, offers excellent dining and lodging for skiers wishing to access Bozeman, Big Sky, and West Yellowstone trails. Bozeman restaurants include Spanish Peaks, John Bozeman's Bistro, and O'Brien's, as well as old favorites like the Rocky Mountain Pasta Company and the Baucus Pub. Bridger Bowl's Jim Bridger Lodge has cafeteria food and Jimmy Bs sit-down dining. Ski equipment is also available in Bozeman at Bangtail and Northern Lights.
Phone numbers:	Bohart Ranch Cross Country Ski Center (406) 586–9070. Bozeman Ranger District (406) 522–2520. Bridger Bowl Ski Area central reservations (800) 223–9609. Bozeman Area Chamber of Commerce (800) 228–4224; (406) 586–5421. Gallatin Gateway Inn (800) 676–3522. Silver Forest Inn (888) 835–5970. Bangtail (406) 587–4905. Northern Lights (406) 586–2225. Emergency 911 alerts the sheriff. Cell phones work intermittently. Avalanche information (406) 587–6981.

Bohart Ranch sits in the historic and rugged Bridger Canyon below the Bridger Mountain Range. The Bridgers are named for mountain man Jim Bridger, who led wagons to Bozeman and nearby gold prospecting areas in the 1860s. The Bohart Ranch trails wind through meadows and forest on both private and Forest Service land.

From the ski hut, ski west to Bohart Loop, a 3-kilometer trail suitable for intermediates. The trail climbs and accesses the rest of the trail

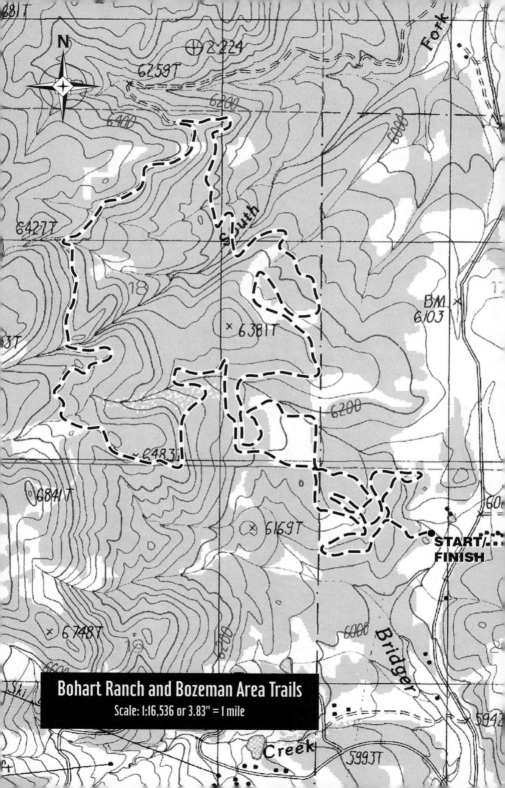

N

2 224

6259T

6200

6400

6427T

South

18

6381T

BM 6103

6483T

6200

6841T

6169T

START/
FINISH

6748T

6200

Bridger

6000

Bohart Ranch and Bozeman Area Trails
Scale: 1:16,536 or 3.83" = 1 mile

Creek

5993T

5942

system via Jane's Gate and either Inner or Outer Meadow Loops. Separate snowshoe trails are ungroomed leaving from the warming hut. Snowshoers are welcome on the ski trails' skate lane but not on the classic tracks.

A more challenging trail from the Meadow Loops begins with the Bracket Creek ski to Logger Loop Trail, with several hills and the intimidating-sounding Bloody Gulch route, which is more fun than scary. Skiers can complete a large loop of the entire area by skiing past Bloody Gulch, crossing Brackett Creek, and turning right/north on the 5-kilometer Logger's Loop. The trail climbs through timbered terrain, looping south and along the base of the Bridger Mountain Range. Skiers may choose the new This Way to Norway Loop off Logger's for an additional 2 kilometers. The entire outer trail ski is 15 kilometers from the trailhead. Skiers return to the trailhead on the remainder of Logger's Loop heading east. The steep downhill offers a challenge but once skiers reach Meadow Loop and turn right/east, the terrain becomes rolling hills to the trailhead.

Bohart's Biathlon Range is unique and popular. The range opens to biathletes for scheduled target practice and competitions. Another biathlon practice range is available for regular use; sign-in and a fee are required. Bohart hosts several annual ski events, including the Bridger Mountain Tour in January and the North American Cup Biathlon in February. During the summer the Bohart trails are open for running, biking, and horse riding (bring your own steed) and as a Disc Golf course.

Numerous backcountry ski and snowshoe opportunities in the Boze-

Directions at a glance
From the parking area, pick up a trail pass in the wood hut. Trails leave the hut heading south or west.

man area are listed with the Bozeman Ranger District Office. A local favorite is the ski from Bear Canyon to Bear Lakes or to Mystic Lake. These popular ski-touring routes are not recommended for beginners due to climbs and length. The trail to Bear Lakes from Bear Canyon Road begins where the road dead-ends and becomes Trail 440. The trail is packed by snowmobiles for the 6 miles to Bear Lakes. It climbs southeast; the return is by the same route. It is moderate to difficult climbing on snow-covered roads and trails mostly in timbered terrain. Skiers should use edged skis.

A popular skiers-only trail leaves Bear Canyon on the New World Gulch Trail to Mystic Lake. Drive 3.5 miles on Bear Canyon and look for the New World Gulch trailhead sign on the southwest side of the road at the large parking area. The 5.5-mile New World Gulch Trail begins at 5,440 feet elevation and follows a creek south on a steady and sometimes steep uphill. The trail leaves the creek past the Forest Service gate and follows open meadows before climbing through lodgepole pines and spruce to the ridge top between New World Gulch and the Bozeman Creek drainage. From the ridge, the trail drops down to Mystic Lake at 6,550 feet and follows the east shore to meet the trail to Bozeman Creek. The Mystic Lake recreation cabin is available for rent from the Bozeman Ranger District.

How to get there

Bohart Ranch is 16.6 miles northeast of Bozeman. From Bozeman's Main Street, drive east to Rouse Avenue and turn left/north until it becomes Highway 86. Continue north through Bridger Canyon. Look for the sign for Bridger Bowl Ski Area on the left. Bohart is .8 mile further on the left/west.

Bear Canyon trails are 4.5 miles east of Bozeman on Interstate 90 to the Bear Canyon exit. Drive west for .5 mile to Bear Canyon Road and drive south for 3.5 miles to the New World Gulch parking area.

Lone Mountain Ranch
Big Sky, Montana

Type of trail:	▬ ▬ ⬭ ◁
Also used by:	Nordic skiers and snowshoers only
Distance:	45 miles/75 kilometers
Terrain:	Flat to hilly
Trail difficulty:	Easiest to most challenging
Surface quality:	Machine-groomed daily
Elevation:	6,200 to 8,240 feet
Food and facilities:	Lone Mountain Ranch guests stay, ski, and eat at the ranch. The twenty-three charming and rustic (no phone or TV) trail-side log cabins allow skiers literally to step out the door and onto skis. The award-winning Dining Lodge features Montana delicacies like bison and Montana beef. The small community of Big Sky, ten minutes from the ranch, has all services, including superb cuisine at Edelweiss Restaurant, First Place Restaurant, and the famed Buck's T-4 steak house. Additional lodging, restaurants, and shops are 5 miles west on Big Sky Spur Road at Big Sky Ski and Summer Resort. Lone Mountain's Outdoor Shop rents quality skis and snowshoes. The ranch's PSIA-certified ski instructors offer a full range of workshops for first-timers and experts alike.
Phone numbers:	Lone Mountain Ranch (800) 514–4644. Big Sky Chamber of Commerce (800) 943–4111. Big Sky Ski and Summer Resort (800) 548–4486. Avalanche forecast (406) 587–6981. Emergency 911. Cell phones work intermittently in the mountains.

Lone Mountain Ranch's ski trails are the among finest tracks in the country. The combination of cold snow, impeccable grooming, and a ranch staff ratio of more than one staff person per guest proves why Lone Mountain has long set the standard for guest ranches. Lone Mountain began operating over two decades ago in the Spanish Peaks of south-central Montana. In that time, the ranch has become known for not only the 75 kilometers of trails, but also for some of the best dining in the state. Although guests generally stay at the ranch for a week, skiers can opt for day ski trips or sightseeing into Yellowstone National Park, thirty minutes away. Other winter activities include winter fly fishing, sleigh-ride dinners to the North Fork Cabin, and alpine skiing at nearby Big Sky Ski and Summer Resort.

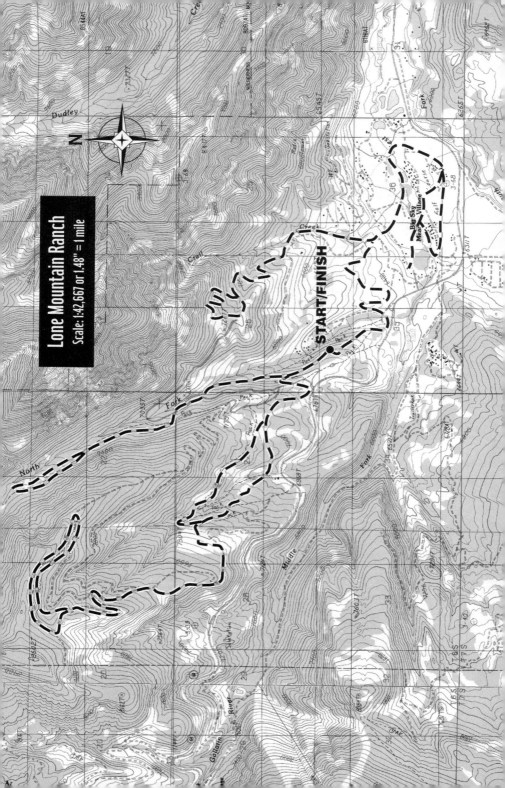

With twenty ski trails, it's difficult to describe all routes, but be assured that the ranch offers over half the trails groomed for intermediate skiers. Skiers looking for relatively flat terrain should try Silverbow and Yellowstone loops, located in Meadow Village. Guests can ski to the area via the Ranch Loop, leaving the Outdoor Shop and skiing south and east 5 kilometers to the Country Store in Meadow Village. The other option is to take a ranch shuttle or drive the 2 miles to the Meadow Village and park at the Country Store. The Yellowstone Loop, located on the golf course, is a 3-kilometer route offering beginner terrain. Silverbow is the northern loop in the Meadow Village area and is a favorite 3-kilometer trail, great for practicing flat-track technique.

For the fit and fast, altitude-loving skaters and kick-n-gliders, the ranch offers a variety of longer routes that climb to 8,240 feet from the ranch at 6,700 feet. The Siberia Trail takes off from the Outdoor Shop heading northwest along the Ranch Loop to North Fork, Dutch's Detour, and Boomerang. There is good signage along the route. This tour winds in and out of meadows and trees as it climbs. Siberia offers superb views of Lone Mountain and some of the Spanish Peaks. The entire ski is a 22-kilometer round trip.

A bit gentler yet spectacular trail is Little Bavaria, an 11-kilometer round trip from the ranch. Skiers begin at the Outdoor Shop on the Ranch Loop, then follow the east side of North Fork Creek. This trail intersects Little Bavaria at 2 kilometers. From here, the 5-kilometer Little Bavaria follows the creek toward the Spanish Peaks. Exciting downhills run through open meadows. The view of 9,442-foot Yellow Mountain makes carrying a camera worthwhile.

Snowshoes are not allowed on ski trails; however, four separate snowshoe trails total 10 kilometers. Snowshoers should take the 1.5-mile/2.4-kilometer Nature Trail, which leaves from the Outdoor Shop heading west and then north. The trail passes the Bull Moose guest cabin before looping back along a ridge top, through the ranch cabins, and to the Outdoor Shop. The 2-mile/3.2 kilometer Ralph's Outlook loop takes off from the Nature Trail just after crossing a ski trail called Carlin's Cruise. Snowshoers turn north at the sign and climb to 7,200 feet and past a private residence before looping back to the Nature Trail and finally the Outdoor Shop.

How to get there

The ranch is about an hour's drive from Bozeman. Shuttle vehicles make several trips daily from the Bozeman airport for a fee. From downtown Bozeman, take Highway 84 west 7 miles to the Four Corners junction with U.S. 191. Turn left/south onto U.S. 191 and drive 35 miles through Gallatin Canyon. Use caution as this road can get very icy. At the community of Big Sky, turn right on Big Sky Spur Road. The entrance to Lone Mountain Ranch is 4 miles ahead and on the right/north.

Directions at a glance

From behind the ranch's Outdoor Shop at the parking area, trails depart northwest on the Ranch Loop, which accesses the bulk of the trail system. Trail maps and trail passes are available in the Outdoor Shop.

Mountain Meadows Guest Ranch
Big Sky, Montana

Type of trail:	=== ⬭ ◄
Also used by:	An occasional moose
Distance:	18 miles/30 kilometers
Terrain:	Rolling hills to hilly and open meadows
Trail difficulty:	Easiest to moderate
Surface quality:	Groomed single track, skate lane, and snowshoe trails
Elevation:	7,000 to 7,600 feet
Food and facilities:	Guests at the luxurious Mountain Meadows receive all meals, lodging, transportation, trail passes, ski and snowshoe rentals, alpine ski tickets, and a day in Yellowstone for one per-person rate, with a three-day minimum stay. Day skiers are welcome and pay a trail fee. Services including excellent restaurants, saloons, shops, and gas in Big Sky, 9 miles away.
Phone numbers:	Mountain Meadows Guest Ranch (888) 644–6647 or (406) 995–4997. Big Sky Chamber of Commerce (800) 943–4111. Avalanche forecast (406) 587–6981. Emergency 911. Cell phones work intermittently in the mountains.

The 10,000-square-foot log lodge, built in 1999 by the Charles and Eran Severn family, seems like it's on top of the world. This wilderness retreat hosts up to twenty guests in seven guest rooms and one cabin. The family-run operation devotes its entire 580 acres to the guest-ranching business. In summer, there's hiking, biking, Yellowstone trips, horseback riding, fly fishing, rafting, golfing, and swimming. By winter, the lodge feels snowed in, yet is only a twenty-minute, 12-mile drive from the town of Big Sky. Day skiers should plan on staying for dinner in the elegant dining room (reservations necessary) for hearty Montana fare, such as elk medallions, bison, and prime rib. The ski and snowshoe trails were designed with beginners and lessons in mind on the Big EZ Loop, and for seasoned skiers on the more challenging Mountain Meadows Loop and Grizzly Getaway.

Beginners enjoy the 3-kilometer Moose Meadows Loop, named for the two resident bull moose that frequent both the trail and the meadows on either side of the trail. Note that moose and other wildlife are unpredictable and can be dangerous. Do not approach or chase them! From the lodge, Moose Meadows Loop begins at the trailhead sign heading north and loops east past the cabins with few hills. At 1 kilometer, the Spanish Peaks and Lone Mountain offer a backdrop for photos of the ranch.

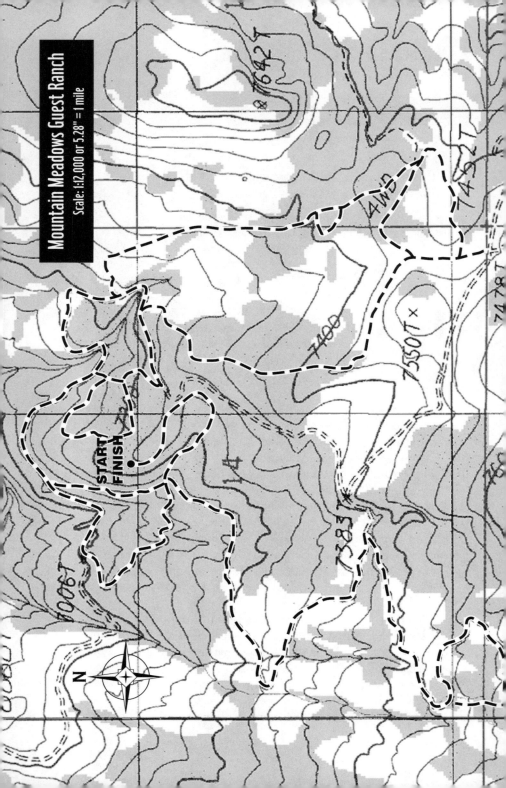

Mountain Meadows Guest Ranch
Scale: 1:12,000 or 5.28" = 1 mile

Kids love Barn Boulevard, an 8-kilometer ski that includes a stop at the barn to see the horses, llamas, donkeys, and other farm animals. From the lodge, skiers start on the Moose Meadows Trail, skiing east 1 kilometer to the Mountain Meadows Loop trails. At 1 kilometer, the trail connects with Barn Boulevard, then heads up to the barn. Skiers can return on the same trail for a total of 8 kilometers out and back, or continue to Big EZ for a longer trip.

Past the barn 1 kilometer is the intersection with the Big EZ 3-kilometer loop. Skiers can either take Big EZ heading north or south and connect with Chuck's Hillside Heaven. Here is a good place to try telemarking among the open glades. Skiers can either telemark down the wide-open glade and connect back with the lower Mountain Meadow Loop, or hike back up to Chuck's Hillside Heaven to finish on the Mountain Meadow's Loop back to the lodge.

The exhilarating climb on Lookout Loop is worth every one of the 14 kilometers. There are expansive views of all of Big Sky, Lone Mountain, Pioneer and Cedar Mountains, all the way to the Spanish Peaks. The other reward for the 400-foot elevation gain is taking a break at the tipi on top of the Lookout Loop trail. If you're skiing with an instructor or guide, there'll be hot chocolate awaiting your arrival at the tipi. The final reward is a pleasant downhill back to the lodge. To access Lookout Loop from the lodge, skiers take Mountain Meadows 3 kilometers and turn east for .5 kilometer to the tipi at Lookout Loop.

How to get there

The ranch is an hour's drive from Bozeman. The best option is taking the ranch shuttle from the Bozeman/Belgrade airport. From the airport, take Highway 191 south. At Four Corners junction continue on U.S. 191 south and drive 36 miles through Gallatin Canyon. Use caution as this road can get very icy. Pass the community of Big Sky and Buck's T-4restaurant/hotel. Immediately after the Ophir School, turn right/west on Beaver Creek Road. Drive 6 miles, staying on the main, plowed road to the log entrance overhang sign to Mountain Meadows Ranch. Continue straight ahead 1.5 miles to the lodge.

Centennial Mountains/Hellroaring Ski Adventures
West Yellowstone, Montana

Type of trail: ▬▬▬

Also used by: Alpine touring skiers and snowboarders

Distance: 2,000 to 4,000 vertical feet per day

Terrain: Mountainous

Trail difficulty: Expert

Surface quality: Untracked powder

Elevation: 6,800 to 10,200 feet

Food and facilities: The Nemesis Mountain Hut is the only facility for 30 miles. The hut is available for rent both by guided parties and by groups of experienced skiers who have previously been guided in the area. Most skiers spend a few nights in West Yellowstone, where all services are available. West Yellowstone's Free Heel and Wheel rents and sells ski equipment.

Phone numbers: Hellroaring Ski Adventures (406) 646–4571 or www.skihellroaring.com. West Yellowstone Chamber of Commerce (406) 646–7701. Free Heel and Wheel (406) 646–7744. West Yellowstone Conference Hotel (800) 646–7365. Transportation from the Bozeman airport from 4x4 Stage (800) 517–8243. Avalanche advisory (406) 587–6981. Emergency 911. Cell phones work intermittently.

The Centennial Mountains of southern Montana were named for the centennial year, 1876, in which cattle were first introduced in the Centennial Valley. The area is best known for the Red Rock Lakes National Wildlife Refuge. The mountains run east-west on the Idaho border and along the Continental Divide.

Expert telemarkers, alpine-touring skiers, and snowboarders who ride split boards find the Hellroaring drainage of the Centennial Mountains an impressive backcountry experience. Note that snowboarders must use a split board or approach skis, not snowshoes. Climbing skins are required. Untracked snow in wide-open bowls, protected powder fields, and unlimited tree skiing lures skiers to high-mountain tours in the Centennials.

The Nemesis Mountain Hut, named for the 9,449-foot Nemesis Mountain, is a custom-built shelter with two large wall tents. Skylights let in the Montana winter sun and provide views to Mt. Jefferson from inside. The bunkroom has room for six skiers. The cooking tent includes two bunks, a small oven on the woodstove, a two-burner propane stove, and all utensils and cooking supplies.

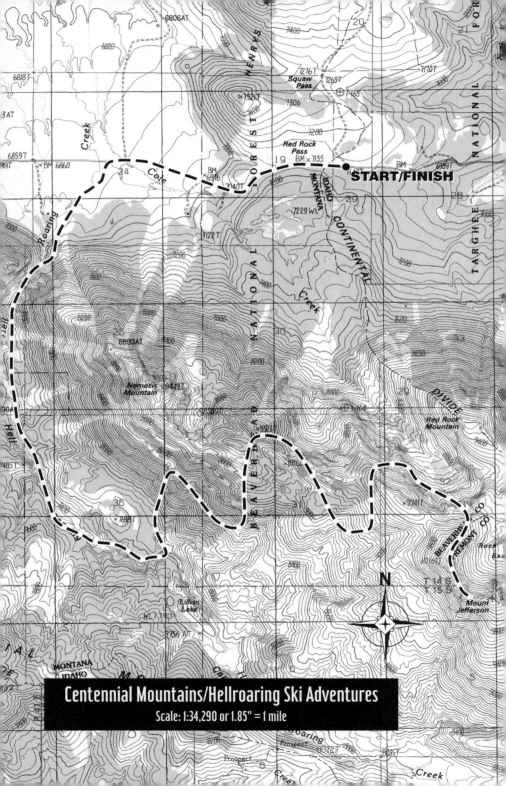

START/FINISH

Centennial Mountains/Hellroaring Ski Adventures
Scale: 1:34,290 or 1.85" = 1 mile

Hellroaring Ski Adventures offers several types of trips. The fully guided trip includes the shuttle, guide, great food prepared by the guide, avalanche rescue equipment, climbing skins, ski instruction, backcountry skills instruction, and hut accommodations. A guided trip includes the ski guide but skiers bring and prepare their own chow. The hut rental is available to experienced skiers who have been on a guided trip to Nemesis Hut in the past. The experienced party must have a trip leader proficient in route finding, avalanche awareness, first aid, bivouac, and evacuation skills.

From the hut a favorite route is the ski up Highlife Point at 9,741 feet.

The climb from the hut is a mellow but steady ninety-minute ascent. The climb passes an old miner's cabin, two long switchbacks, and the top of Miner's Knob. The final 400 feet is among snowghosts (rime-encrusted trees) and exposed terrain. The ski down on protected, west-facing slopes offers 1,000 feet of vertical with steeps ranging from upper 20-degree slopes to lower 30s. The high-mountain views include Mt. Jefferson, all of the Hellroaring drainage, nearby Blair Lake, and Yellowstone National Park.

After skiing Highlife, skiers skin up 400 feet to the top of Miner's Knob. The climb includes two long, gentle traverses and twenty minutes of climbing. Once on top, views include Mt. Jefferson, Reas Peak in the Centennials, and the Tetons of Wyoming. The trip down Miner's Knob covers 1,000 vertical feet of wide-open skiing on the 25- to 35-degree slope. The terrain offers a well-protected west-facing aspect where snow remains drier than on south-facing slopes.

The next choice is often the climb up to the Summit of Jefferson. From the bottom of Miner's Knob, skiers climb once again past Miner's, up to Highlife Point, and then continue southeast along a ridge to the ski-able summit of Jefferson at 10,161 feet, just 40 feet below the craggy true summit.

Ten mountain ranges in three states dominate the skyline. They include the Washburn Range and the Tetons in Wyoming, the Pioneer Mountains in Idaho, and the Tobacco Root Mountains and Gravelly Range of Montana. Jefferson's 3,000-foot descent from the summit to the hut is generally the finale for a good day of powder. The top 400 feet can be wind-blown, but below that skiers find powder turns skiing west back to the hut.

How to get there

After meeting your group in West Yellowstone at Free Heel and Wheel, drive 13 miles west on Highway 20. Turn north on Highway 87 and drive to Henry's Lake Road. Turn left/west; drive for 5.3 miles. Park at the dead end at the junction of three unplowed roads. A snowmobile shuttles skiers and gear over the 7,120-foot Red Rock Pass to the trailhead. From the trailhead, ski 3.5 miles to Nemesis Mountain Hut, gaining 1,200 feet of elevation.

Directions at a glance

From the parking lot on the west side of Henry's Lake, look for the snowmobile shuttle on the west side of the parking area.

Rendezvous Ski Trails
West Yellowstone, Montana

Type of trail: ⟍ ◅

Also used by: Trail crosses snowmobile trail; bison

Distance: 18 miles/37.5 kilometers

Terrain: Flat to rolling hills

Trail difficulty: Beginner to advanced

Surface quality: Machine-groomed daily for classic and skate skiing

Elevation: 6,666 to 6,850 feet

Food and facilities: West Yellowstone has all services, although not all restaurants and shops are open in winter. The West Yellowstone Conference Hotel caters to skiers and other winter visitors and is within walking distance of the trailhead. The Chamber of Commerce provides a listing of hotels that are open in winter. Free Heel and Wheel rents and sells ski and snowshoe equipment and has information on trail conditions. Free Wheel also has a friendly coffee bar inside the ski shop. Trails are open and groomed from approximately mid November through the end of March. A warming hut and outhouse are located at the Biathlon Range. Be aware that hundreds of snowmobilers converge on West Yellowstone to enjoy the snowmobile trails in the region. The Rendezvous Ski Trails are closed to snowmobiles.

Phone numbers: Hebgen Lake Ranger District (406) 646–7369. West Yellowstone Chamber of Commerce (406) 646–7701. Free Heel and Wheel (406) 646–7744. West Yellowstone Conference Hotel (800) 646–7365. Ski guiding and lessons, Yellowstone Alpen Guides (406) 646–9591. Avalanche information (406) 646–7912. Emergency 911. Cell phones work intermittently.

Since the establishment of the Rendezvous Ski Trails about 1980, the system has gradually gained a well-deserved national reputation for excellence in trail design, grooming, and ski testing. On some winter days, the trails can provide a feeling of solitude, while at other times special events draw hundred of skiers. The annual Fall Camp Thanksgiving weekend turns the Rendezvous Trails into the training site for the U.S. Nordic and Biathlon Ski Teams. While the fastest U.S. skiers skate and glide the forested trails, many other ski teams train alongside racers in red, white, and blue. Spring's Rendezvous Ski Race also draws hundreds of racers for the 50-kilometer and shorter-distance races. Springtime

Rendezvous Ski Trails

Excellent maps for the Rendezvous Ski Trails are available at the trailhead, the Free Heel and Wheel Ski Shop, the Forest Service Office, and the West Yellowstone Chamber of Commerce. These trails are one of the best signed trails in the state—there are signs at every intersection.

"crust cruising"—skiing on early-morning, hard-pack snow—is a locally favorite tour.

Before skiing, purchase the required day trail pass from the self-service pay station at the trailhead, or buy a season pass at the Chamber of Commerce office, one of the ski shops, or at the Hebgen Lake Ranger District Office.

From the trailhead, the Approach Trail begins with the flat .9-kilometer Kid's Loop, which includes the kid-magnet Kid's Hill. Other trails are accessed via the 1.2-kilometer Approach Trail. From under the log arch sign, ski south 100 meters and then turn right/west and follow the groomed tracks through the lodgepole forest. At about a quarter of a kilometer, the Kid's Hill looms at the right edge of the trail. Herringbone tracks lead to the top of this small mound. Kids love doing laps here, climbing up, racing down, sometimes crashing, and repeating the fun. The rest of the Kid's Loop makes left turns at the next three junctions, all of them well marked, to return to the parking area.

The rest of the 29 kilometers are accessed by turning right/west at the Bison Boulevard junction, .3 kilometer into Kid's Loop. Ski .6 kilometer to the next junction and turn right/west again, and cross the South Plateau Snowmobile Trail. During the many ski camps and races, numerous ski company representatives park at the junction referred to as "the corral," with the snowmobile trail and offer ski equipment demos. From here the ski trail choices include an interesting route along the Biathlon Range, a must-see if an event is scheduled. Ski .18 kilometer to Rendezvous Junction and stay to the right, following the signs and perhaps the sounds of rifle shots, another .37 kilometer to the Biathlon Range. Watch for racers here doing laps on the course.

For more challenging terrain, skiers find the most difficult trails of the 2.3-kilometer Volunteer Loop or the 8.3-kilometer Windy Ridge Loop. The Volunteer Loop is a good choice for blustery days. It departs from Rendezvous Junction heading southeast on hilly terrain, finally meeting up with Rendezvous Loop, where skiers can return to Rendezvous Junction by following the trail signs north. Rendezvous offers several cutoff loops to return to the trailhead or ski longer distances.

Windy Ridge Loop is generally ungroomed and an exciting route for experienced skiers wanting an all-day ski. Downhill sections and scenic vistas reward skiers on this difficult trail. Skiers should definitely take food and water and plan on a few hours up here. From Rendezvous Junction, several options exist to access Windy Ridge. The most direct option is to ski to Rendezvous Loop and then to Dead Dog Loop, and at Junction 13 turn right/west onto Windy Ridge. This large loop can be windy and may have wind-blown crust or snowed-in tracks. It's recommended to check conditions at one of the ski shops before going. Windy Ridge meets up with Dead Dog Loop again for a long trek back to the trailhead, following signs to Rendezvous Junction. This route provides views into the Gallatin Mountain Range and Yellowstone National Park.

How to get there

From West Yellowstone, the trails begin in town. Drive west on Yellowstone Avenue (which is also the entrance to Yellowstone National Park) and turn left/south on Geyser Street. Drive 1 block and park at the intersection of Geyser Street and Obsidian Avenue in the plowed parking area.

Directions at a glance

From the parking area, the trailhead is under the overhanging log sign, Rendezvous Ski Trails, heading south.

Riverside Ski Trail
Yellowstone National Park

Type of trail: ▬▬▬

Also used by: Moose, elk, bison

Distance: 5 miles/8.4 kilometers

Terrain: Flat except for a few short hills

Trail difficulty: Easy

Surface quality: Intermittently machine-groomed

Elevation: 6,666 to 6,690 feet

Food and facilities: West Yellowstone has all services, although not all restaurants and shops are open in winter. The West Yellowstone Conference Hotel caters to skiers and other winter visitors and is within walking distance to the trailhead. The Chamber of Commerce provides a list of businesses that are open in winter. For a good, inexpensive dinner, try the Old Town Cafe on Madison Avenue and ask about the bison special. Ski equipment is available at Bud Lilly's Trout/Ski Shop and Free Heel and Wheel. Free Heel has information on trail conditions and a friendly coffee bar inside the ski shop. Yellowstone Alpen Guides offers ski lessons and guiding inside the park boundary.

Phone numbers: West Yellowstone Chamber of Commerce (406) 646–7701. Yellowstone National Park headquarters (307) 344–7381. Big Sky Chamber of Commerce (800) 943–4111. Free Heel and Wheel (406) 646–7744. West Yellowstone Conference Hotel (800) 646–7365. Ski guiding and skier transportation inside Yellowstone available from Yellowstone Alpen Guides (406) 646–9591. Transportation from the Bozeman airport from 4x4 Stage (800) 517–8243. Avalanche advisory (406) 587–6981. Emergency 911 or Yellowstone National Park Communications Center (307) 344–7381 + 0. Cell phones work intermittently.

The Riverside Ski Trail crosses very easy terrain. New skiers can try out the sport and ski to impressive views inside America's first national park. No snowshoes or skate skiers here. Locals send families and photographers on this trail, which glides along the Montana portion of the Madison River just inside Yellowstone's boundary. Views include the 10,336-foot Mt. Holmes and the Gallatin Mountain Range. Bison, elk, and moose frequent the river area and sometimes use the packed trail.

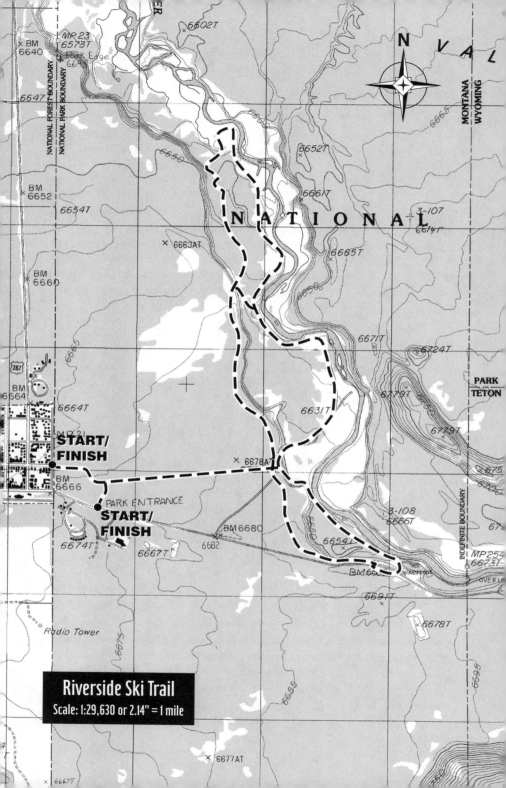

Riverside Ski Trail
Scale: 1:29,630 or 2.14" = 1 mile

Keep a safe distance from all wildlife. Winter is a difficult time for the animals. Don't try to make them move off a trail—just ski around the wildlife.

From the trailhead, ski east along a one-track route. After a quarter mile, there is a trail registration post. At this point, the trail joins with another short trail coming in from the south. This simply is another trailhead from the West Entrance Road; however, the Boundary Street trailhead is the better choice to avoid snowmobiles on the park road.

Continue east on a very straight trail that follows under telephone wires. Called the Cutoff Trail, the first mile begins in a dense lodgepole forest. The next junction provides views across the Madison River basin. A few orange trail markers line the route and are nailed to trees.

The Upriver Loop is a 2.5-kilometer trail that begins by crossing the ski trail and climbing up a short way to the overlook above the river's wide valley. From here you can catch a glimpse of the destruction wrought by the Yellowstone fires of 1988. Turn right/south and ski along the river's shoulder. The river is wide here and the water channel may be dry next to the trail and filled beyond the next river shoulder east. Don't ski out on the ice. The trail continues south and east and includes a brief downhill slope. The trail will climb up the bank again before turning back. After 1.2 kilometers, the trail loops back west and then north 1.3 kilometers and meets the Cutoff Trail and the Downriver Loop. Skiers can either return to the trailhead or continue north for another 5.9-kilometer loop.

The popular Downriver Loop rambles past lodgepole forests to flat commutes along the river. From the Upriver Loop, head north and along the river bench. The trail takes a short downhill to the riverbed and follows the river path. At about 1.8 kilometers, another cutoff shortcut allows skiers to avoid the full 5.9 kilometers. The hill climb here to the shortcut is short but steep. With either the shortcut or the full Downriver Loop, there is a short hill. Beginners uncomfortable with the climb and descent might side-step the hill. The return trip ambles along an easy route back to the trailhead cutoff, where skiers turn west for the final 1.6 kilometers.

How to get there

The Riverside Ski Trail is within walking distance of most hotels in West Yellowstone. From the Highway 191 and Yellowstone Avenue intersection, head north 1 block, and turn right/east on Madison Avenue. One block later, the street ends on Boundary Street. Park here and walk across Boundary Street to the trailhead.

Directions at a glance

The trailhead is on the east edge of the intersection of Boundary Street and Madison Avenue. Look for the orange trail sign and for skiers' tracks heading east into the woods.

Upper Madison Valley Trail
Yellowstone National Park

Type of trail: ▬▬▬ ⬭

Also used by: Elk, bison, bears

Distance: 14 miles/22.4 kilometers

Terrain: Flat with a few ridges

Trail difficulty: Most difficult

Surface quality: Skier-packed

Elevation: 6,600 to 6,820 feet

Food and facilities: The closest community is West Yellowstone, 9.5 miles south. West Yellowstone's Free Heel and Wheel rents and sells ski and snowshoe equipment and can offer trail conditions and ski lessons. Yellowstone National Park has trail information and hiking maps. Winter camping is allowed in the park. Overnighters are required to obtain a free backcountry use permit, available at the West Yellowstone Entrance Ranger Station, daytime only. Yellowstone Alpen Guides offers ski guiding into the park.

Phone numbers: West Yellowstone Chamber of Commerce (406) 646–7701. Yellowstone National Park headquarters (307) 344–7381. West Entrance Ranger Station (406) 646–7332. Free Heel and Wheel (406) 646–7744. West Yellowstone Conference Hotel (800) 646–7365. Ski guiding available from Yellowstone Alpen Guides (800) 858–3502 or (406) 646–9591. Transportation from the Bozeman airport available from 4x4 Stage (800) 517–8243. Avalanche advisory (406) 646–7912. Emergency 911 or Yellowstone National Park Communications Center (307) 344–7381 + 0. Cell phones work intermittently.

The Upper Madison Valley Trail, although easily accessible, sees few winter visitors. The trail rewards skiers with views into three states and four mountain ranges, and travelers here may see herds of bison and elk. The 14-mile trail is quite challenging—not because of elevation changes but because route-finding skills are necessary to complete the trail. Additionally, several creek crossings require skiers to remove skis and jump over narrow creeks or, at wider creeks, to remove boots and cross barefoot in 2 feet of ice water. Some spots might have downed trees to use as bridges. Locals advise visitors to hire Yellowstone Alpen Guides for this trip. The guides know the route, know the history and geology of the area, and provide a shuttle to the trailhead. Sometimes the trail is

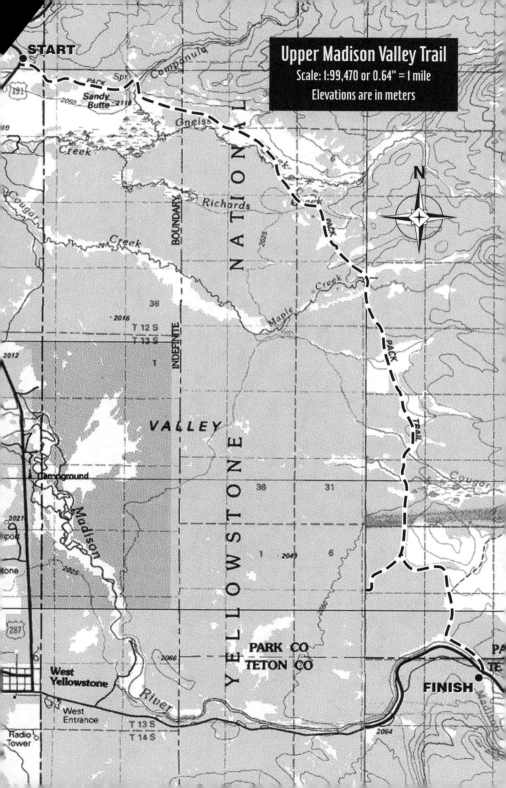

closed in spring for grizzly bear management, so check with the Park Service before leaving for the trailhead. An over-the-snow vehicle shuttle is required for the pick-up at trail's end, and can be arranged with the guides.

From the Fir Ridge parking area near the Fir Ridge Cemetery, the trail leads east into an aspen grove on Forest Service land. Note that locals refer to this trail as the Duck Creek Trail, although the park calls it the Madison Valley Trail or Gneiss Creek Trail. Several fingers of the trail all go in roughly the same direction and meet up within a few hundred yards of the trailhead. Ski on Fir Ridge about .4 mile to the park boundary. At about 2 miles, the trail drops into Campanula Creek and some beaver ponds at 6,600 feet elevation. The trail crosses into Wyoming. Once across Campanula Creek, there's a dimple in the trail. Go north around the beaver ponds. There are vistas west to the Centennial Range and Mt. Sawtelle (which sports a radar tower), and to the Madison Range farther in the distance. Skyline Ridge is to the northwest and the Gallatin Range can be seen to the northeast. There is no thermal activity in the area. This route is the old Bannock Indian trail leading to buffalo-hunting territory on the park's east side.

The trail follows the edge of Burnt Hole Basin, named by the first trappers in the 1820s who observed a fresh burn here. Follow Burnt Hole Basin to a knob and drop into a beaver pond area. There are no bridges so travelers must find logs to cross. It is easy to become lost in the beaver-pond area, a good reason to hire a guide for this trip. Note that most downed trees here point northeast because of the prevailing southwest winds. Burned-out trees from the 1988 fires remain standing here as sculpted black posts. In this large, open meadow area, binoculars are needed to find the orange ski markers, which may be up to .5 mile apart. The markers are either nailed to trees or on posts in the meadows; however, the bison use the posts for scratching and sometimes knock them down.

From Burnt Hole, follow the meadow's eastern edge along open meadows and across several timbered ridges. Stay far away from elk and buffalo: They can be dangerous and should not be stressed by running in deep snow. At 5 miles, cross Gneiss Creek and then Richards Creek. At the halfway point is Maple Creek, where a bridge washed out in 1999 and has not been replaced. Approaching Maple requires skiing down a 150-foot hill. The remainder of the ski is relatively flat all way to the ridge, dropping down to 7-Mile Bridge and the pick-up point.

At 12 miles, and skiing south, a large meadows area opens up east of the trail. This is called Horse Meadows; cavalry troops and stage lines once grazed their horses here. Ski on the west side of the meadows.

Much of the trail here is among lodgepole pines. Just before trail's end, ski through a Douglas fir forest. There is a trail junction at 12.5 miles. Take the left/southeast trail. The final .5 mile follows the north side of the Madison River to 7-Mile Bridge and the Gneiss Trailhead.

How to get there

From West Yellowstone, drive north on Highway 191 for 9.5 miles. Look for the Fir Ridge Cemetery sign and turn right/east just after the sign. Park along the circle turn-around area. An over-the-snow vehicle shuttle must be arranged to pick up skiers at 7-Mile Bridge inside the park.

Directions at a glance

The trail begins on the eastern edge of the parking circle heading east. Several small trails take off here and parallel one another. They meet up a few hundred yards east.

Specimen Creek Trail
Yellowstone National Park

Type of trail: ▰▰▰ ▱▱▱

Also used by: Walkers, wildlife

Distance: 16 miles/25.6 kilometers

Terrain: Gradual climb to steeps with avalanche hazards

Trail difficulty: Moderate to very challenging

Surface quality: Backcountry

Elevation: 6,700 to 9,200 feet

Food and facilities: The closest civilization to the Specimen Creek trailhead is 26.5 miles south in the town of West Yellowstone or 23 miles north in Big Sky. West Yellowstone's Free Heel and Wheel rents and sells ski and snowshoe equipment and can provide information on trail conditions. Yellowstone National Park has some trail information and hiking maps. Winter campers are required to obtain a Backcountry Use Permit. The permits are free of charge and are available at the West Yellowstone Entrance Ranger Station, daytime only.

Phone numbers: Cell phones work intermittently. West Yellowstone Chamber of Commerce (406) 646–7701. Yellowstone National Park headquarters (307) 344–7381. Big Sky Chamber of Commerce (800) 943–4111. Free Heel and Wheel (406) 646–7744. West Yellowstone Conference Hotel (800) 646–7365. Ski guiding available from Yellowstone Alpen Guides (406) 646–9591. Transportation from the Bozeman airport provided by 4x4 Stage (800) 517–8243. Emergency 911 or Yellowstone National Park Communications Center (307) 344–7381 + 0. Avalanche advisory (406) 587–6981.

Specimen Creek to Shelf Lake is a popular ski route. Most winter visitors track out and back in a day rather than winter camp. Climbing skins and avalanche gear are necessary for some steep sections 7 miles from the trailhead and in the final mile to Shelf Lake. Skiers without such gear and expertise should turn around at the junction to Crescent Lake or before the final mile to Shelf Lake. Most of the Specimen Creek Trail is skiable without metal edged skis unless icy conditions exist. It's that last mile into the lake that makes skiers wish for metal edges and beefy ski boots.

From the trailhead, the first 2 miles follow along the north side of

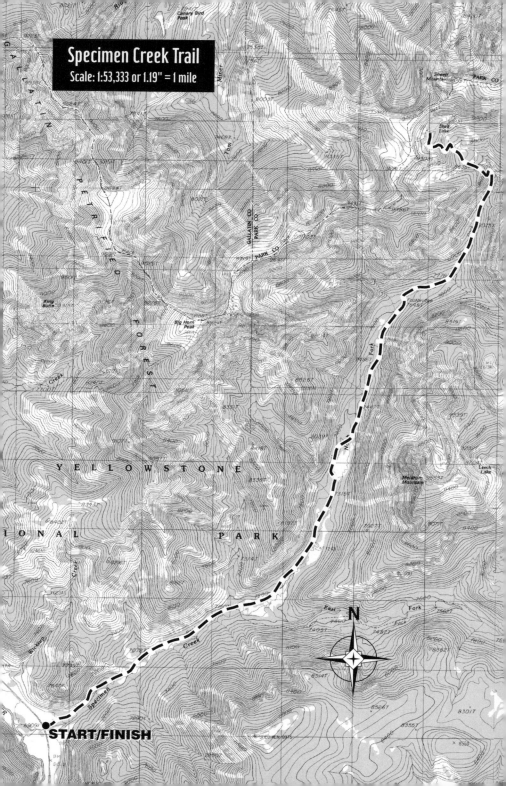

Specimen Creek on rolling, climbing terrain. Skiers pass under a rocky slope, home to marmots and pikas. The aspen grove makes for interesting photography later in the day. Watch for wolves and perhaps a fresh wolf kill in this area. The wolves are part of the packs reintroduced in 1995–1996. Remember that any wild animal can be dangerous and should be enjoyed and photographed from a distance. Elk and moose also frequent the area. The petrified trees on exposed ridges in this area are an especially interesting feature. The petrified trees are the remains of a forest that was engulfed by lava in one of the many volcanic eruptions that have occurred for millions of years in Yellowstone. Buried trees absorbed silica from the mud and ash to become preserved.

At 2 miles, the Sportsman Lake junction takes off right/east and could be an alternative route. Sportsman Lake is 9 miles from here on a challenging trail.

Shelf Lake skiers continue north on the North Fork of Specimen Creek. The trail climbs gradually through timber and meadows. At 4 miles is the trail junction for Crescent Lake, another possible side trip. Crescent Lake is 1 mile west on a steep trail where climbing skins and avalanche gear are recommended. Crescent Lake is located in an impressive mountain cirque, although getting there requires climbing another 850 feet in 1 mile.

From the trail junction with Crescent Lake, the route to Shelf Lake heads north 2 miles, ascending 1,400 feet. Due north is Sheep Mountain at 10,095 feet, sporting large communications relaying equipment. To the west is Bighorn Peak, 9,930 feet high. The park's northern boundary is just north of Shelf Lake on the obvious ridge line above the lake to Sheep Mountain. The final mile into Shelf Lake is considered to have moderate to severe avalanche hazards. Climbing skins and avalanche gear are recommended for skiing the last mile into Shelf Lake. Skiers lacking skins should turn around and return to the Specimen Creek trailhead.

How to get there
From West Yellowstone, drive 26.5 miles north on Highway 191. The trailhead is a plowed parking area at milepost 27, on the east side of the highway. A large trailhead sign is visible from the road. Driving from the north, the trailhead is 5 miles inside the northern park boundary.

Directions at a glance
The trail begins behind the trailhead sign heading east.

Fawn Pass
Yellowstone National Park

Type of trail:	▬▬▬ ▦▦▦
Also used by:	Hikers, wildlife
Distance:	22 miles/35.2 kilometers
Terrain:	Gradual to steeper climbs and downhills with avalanche hazards
Trail difficulty:	Moderate
Surface quality:	Backcountry
Elevation:	7,200 to 9,100 feet
Food and facilities:	The closest town to the Fawn Pass Trailhead is West Yellowstone, 22 miles south, or Big Sky, 18 miles north. West Yellowstone's Free Heel and Wheel rents and sells ski and snowshoe equipment and can provide ski lessons and information on trail conditions. Yellowstone National Park has some trail information and hiking maps. Winter camping is allowed in the park. Overnighters are required to obtain a free Backcountry Use Permit available at the West Yellowstone Entrance Ranger Station, daytime only. Yellowstone Alpen Guides offers ski guiding into the park.
Phone numbers:	West Yellowstone Chamber of Commerce (406) 646–7701. Yellowstone headquarters (307) 344–7381. Big Sky Chamber of Commerce (800) 943–4111. Free Heel and Wheel (406) 646–7744. West Yellowstone Conference Hotel (800) 646–7365. Ski guiding available from Yellowstone Alpen Guides (406) 646–9591. Transportation from the Bozeman airport from 4x4 Stage (800) 517–8243. Avalanche advisory (406) 587–6981. Emergency 911 or Yellowstone National Park Communications Center (307) 344–7381 + 0. Cell phones work intermittently.

Fawn Pass begins in Montana and enters Wyoming after crossing several fingers of the Gallatin River. Skiers find narrow snow bridges or log bridges over these streams and may want to carry skis across. The streams are not deep but they are very cold! This scenic area is prime moose habitat; watch for moose especially in the brush along the streams. The trail area is also home to grizzly bears, black bears, elk, deer, and a veritable Noah's Ark of other wildlife. Although bears generally are sleeping the winter away, they have been seen every month of the year. Bears tend to be a bit groggy during the winter months.

For the first 5 miles, this trail climbs gradually to the Bighorn Pass

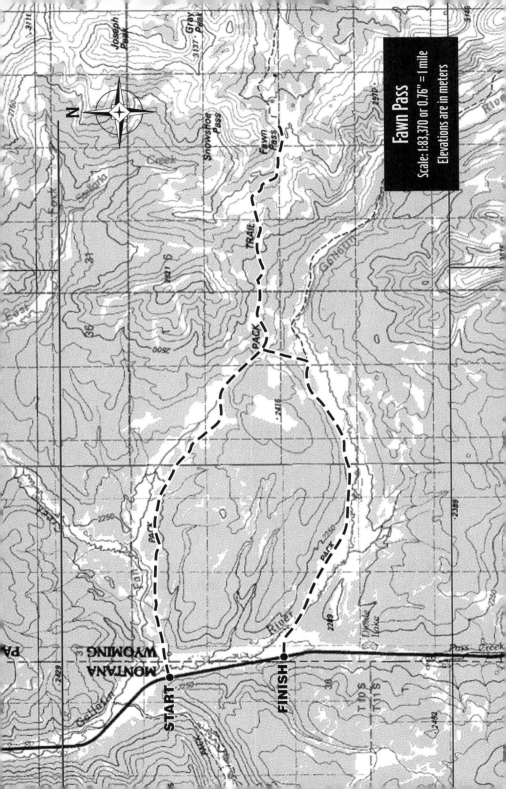

Cutoff Trail. Two miles from the trailhead is the Fan Creek trail junction heading north. Remain on the Fawn Pass Trail (east), and look for evidence of the 1974 forest fire that cleaned out the large trees here. New growth is evident by the two- to three-story-tall evergreens.

The Fawn Pass Trail to Bighorn Pass Trail makes a fine touring loop back to Highway 191. It connects with Fawn Pass Trail, which ends at the Bighorn trailhead, for a total of 10.5 miles. This trip requires hitchhiking back to the Fawn Pass trailhead or using shuttle vehicles. To com-

plete this loop, after 5 miles on the Fawn Pass Trail, turn right/south at the trail junction onto Bighorn Pass Cutoff Trail. Be aware that there are a few switchbacks on this 1-mile trek down to the Bighorn Pass Trail.

Once on the Bighorn Pass Trail, head right/west and back to Highway 191. This trail traverses meadow areas and provides views of places burned in the wildfires of 1988, which scorched 793,880 acres, 36 percent of the park. The stark reminders of the fire are balanced by evidence of rejuvenation in the form of countless new-growth trees. This ski down gently loses elevation from 7,600 to 7,200 feet.

Those wishing to ski on to Fawn Pass at 9,100 feet should be competent on steeper grades both uphill and down. Climbing skins may be necessary in icy conditions. The avalanche hazard increases 2 miles after the junction with Bighorn Pass Trail as the elevation increases, and is especially troublesome closer to Fawn Pass.

At the top of Fawn Pass is a small frozen lake that feeds Fawn Creek, which flows east. The trail continues on to meet the Mammoth/Norris Road, a total of 21.5 miles one-way. This trip would involve arranging a shuttle to the east Fawn Pass trailhead, 2.5 miles south of the community of Mammoth.

How to get there

From West Yellowstone, the trailhead is 22 miles north on Highway 191. The parking area is on the east side of the highway and is well marked. If using a shuttle vehicle to ski to the Fawn Pass/Bighorn loop, park at the Bighorn trailhead, 1.5 miles south of the Fawn Pass parking area, on the east side of Highway 191.

Directions at a glance

From the large plowed parking area the trail is visible to the east down a steep bank. Easiest is to side-step down the bank on the north end of the parking area, then head east on the trail.

Daly Creek to Black Butte Trailhead
Yellowstone National Park

Type of trail: ▬▬▬ ●●●

Also used by: Winter hikers

Distance: 6.5 miles/10.4 kilometers

Terrain: Gradual climbs to mountainous

Trail difficulty: Moderate

Surface quality: Skier-tracked

Elevation: 6,600 to 7,600 feet

Food and facilities: Big Sky is 17 miles north of the trailhead and has all services. Excellent dining spots include First Place Restaurant and Edelweiss Restaurant. Lodging choices include Lone Mountain Ranch, Buck's T-4 Best Western, and the Rainbow Ranch Lodge. West Yellowstone has all services, although not all restaurants and shops are open in winter. The West Yellowstone Conference Hotel caters to skiers and other winter visitors and is within walking distance of the trailhead. The Chamber of Commerce provides a listing of businesses that are open in winter. Ski equipment is available at Bud Lilly's Trout/Ski Shop and Free Heel and Wheel. Free Heel provides information on trail conditions, tips for beginners, and a friendly coffee bar inside the ski shop. Yellowstone Alpen Guides offers ski lessons and guiding inside the park.

Phone numbers: Emergency 911 or Yellowstone National Park Communications Center (307) 344–7381 + 0. Cell phones work intermittently. West Yellowstone Chamber of Commerce (406) 646–7701. Park headquarters (307) 344–7381. Big Sky Chamber of Commerce (800) 943–4111. Free Heel and Wheel (406) 646–7744. West Yellowstone Conference Hotel (800) 646–7365. For ski guiding and skier transportation inside Yellowstone call Yellowstone Alpen Guides (406) 646–9591. Transportation from the Bozeman airport is available from 4x4 Stage (800) 517–8243. Avalanche advisory (406) 587–6981.

Just 1 mile inside the northwestern corner of Yellowstone, the Daly Creek Trail is home to elk, wolves, and other Yellowstone natives. This area is popular with elk because it is in a snow shadow, receiving less snow than other parts of the region. The elk have an easier time in the shallower snow than they do in the deeper drifts typical of other

drainages. In the 1960s, the Park Service rounded up elk here to regulate the elk population. Although that is not current park policy, the corral left over from the elk roundup remains.

For skiers, Daly Creek Trail may not be the best choice due to thin snow cover intermittently during the winter. Snowshoers, however, will find the travel relatively easy. The rewards for traveling here include possible wolf sightings, and visitors should be on the lookout for recent elk carcasses—the leftovers from wolf kills. Check with the park rangers in West Yellowstone for information on recent wolf activity. Also check to see if the Black Butte portion of this loop is open for winter travel. The Black Butte trail may be periodically closed to protect wintering wildlife.

From the trailhead, the route winds east along the northern bank of little Daly Creek. The first 1.9 miles climb gently through open meadows with a backdrop of the Gallatin Mountain Range. Photo opportunities include rocky backdrops and dramatic stands of aspen trees. The trail junction at 1.9 miles leads south on the cutoff trail to Black Butte Trail. Trekkers may opt to turn around and retrace their steps back to the Daly Creek trailhead for a 3.8-mile roundtrip. The continued loop to the Black Butte trailhead follows the cutoff trail right/south for 2 miles to the Black Butte Trail. The Daly Creek Trail continues up Daly Creek for 4 miles to the Daly Rims and the park's northern boundary, but it is not recommended as a winter trail. Beyond the cutoff trail, the Daly Creek Trail is difficult to follow and it crosses dangerous avalanche terrain.

From the junction, travel south on the cutoff trail for 2 miles to the junction with the Black Butte Trail. Upon meeting the Black Butte Trail, stay to the right, heading southwest. To the right/north is the 7,910-foot Lava Butte. The route out loses 760 feet in elevation down to the trailhead on Highway 191. The trail follows the north side of Black Butte Creek and offers several opportunities for telemarking if you're on skis. Black Butte looms to the south of the trail at 8,459 feet. Snow cover can be sparse here, as in the Daly Creek area, so snowshoeing is recommended.

How to get there

From West Yellowstone, the trailhead is 30 miles north on Highway 191. Drive with caution and watch for bison, moose, and elk on the highway. The trailhead sits at a plowed parking area on the east side of the highway. A large trailhead

Directions at a glance

From the trailhead sign, head east, behind the sign and up the drainage. The trail begins on the left/north shoulder of Daly Creek.

sign marks the beginning of the trail on the east side of the parking area. If using two vehicles to shuttle, the Black Butte trailhead and parking are at milepost 28.8, approximately 1.2 miles south of the Daly Creek trailhead.

B Bar Guest Ranch
Emigrant, Montana

Type of trail:	▬ ◉ ◀
Also used by:	Wildlife
Distance:	24 miles/40 kilometers
Terrain:	Gentle to mountainous
Trail difficulty:	Beginner to advanced, with 1,000-foot elevation changes on advanced trails
Surface quality:	Machine-groomed and horse-drawn grooming
Elevation:	6,600 to 7,500 feet
Food and facilities:	There are several warming cabins along the trails. There are also rest rooms or outhouses along the trails and at the trailhead. The ranch provides snowshoes, toboggans, and sleds—but no skis. Equipment rentals are available in Bozeman at Bangtail and Northern Lights, in Livingston at Timber Trails, and in Emigrant at Big Sky Fly & Guides. Ranch guests have meals in the dining room. Paradise Valley neighborhood restaurants include Chatham's Bar and Grill in Livingston and Chico Hot Springs Lodge—renowned for excellent dining and the comforts of its natural hot springs—in Chico. In Bozeman, excellent restaurants include Spanish Peaks, The Bistro, and Uncle Louie's.
Phone numbers:	B Bar Guest Ranch (406) 848–7523. 4x4 Stage (800) 517–8243. Gardiner Ranger District (406) 848–7375. Bangtail (406) 587–4905. Northern Lights (406) 586–2225. Timber Trails (406) 222–9550. Big Sky Fly & Guides (406) 333–4401. Chico Hot Springs Lodge (406) 333–4933. Avalanche advisory (406) 587–6981.

B Bar Ranch is a working cattle operation on the edge of Yellowstone National Park in a scenic, high-mountain basin frequented by moose, bison, elk, wolves, lynx, eagles, and other wildlife. This turn-of-the-century homestead ranch in Tom Miner Basin was once a community with more than thirty families. The ranch owns and manages a conservation herd of Ancient White Park cattle, raises and works Suffolk Punch draft horses, and runs a commercial herd of natural beef cattle on the 9,000 deeded acres and 11,000 acre of national forest.

Winter guests stay in spacious lodge rooms or A-frame cabins and dine on the ranch-grown beef, wild game, organic vegetables from the summer garden, and homemade breads. Families love the 40 kilometers

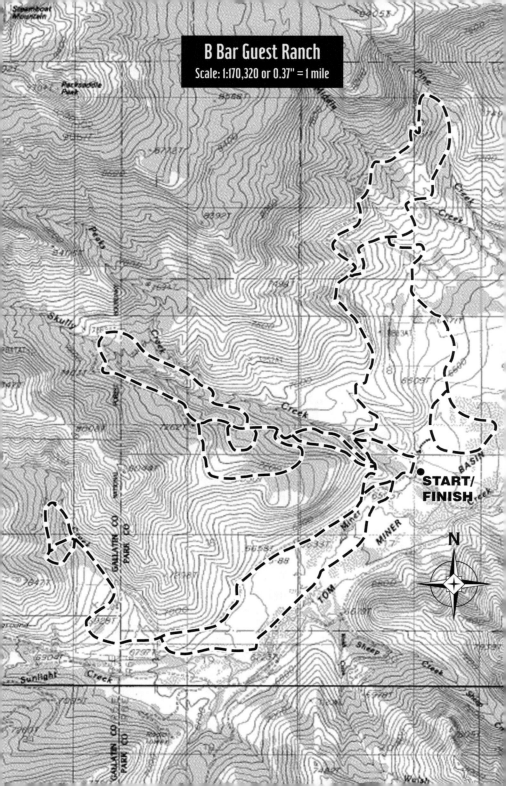

of groomed ski trails and participate in telemarking, snowshoeing, sled-ding, wagon rides, and skijoring. Weekend day skiers are welcome on the trails; a trail fee applies. Nordic ski instructors and guides take skiers and snowshoers on tours of the ranch and reveal its rich natural history. Yel-lowstone Park ski tours in the Lamar Valley and the Tower Falls area can be arranged through the ranch. The ranch's southern boundary is Yel-lowstone National Park.

Beginners enjoy the Anderson Trail, a gentle, 3.5-kilometer route through Tom Miner Basin to the Anderson Cabin. The loop begins at the Nordic tent and heads west through the meadow area. The Anderson Cabin, a rustic and authentic homesteader's log cabin dating from the early 1900s, is 1 kilometer north of the trail and offers views of 9,900-foot Sheep Mountain and Yellowstone National Park. Once skiers pass the cabin, they turn south and then northeast on Willow Way for the return trip.

Skiers can take the more advanced Soldier Creek Trail heading west from the Anderson Cabin cutoff. Soldier Creek Trail climbs to 7,400 feet in 3 kilometers. There are views of Buffalo Horn Pass and 10,289-foot Ramshorn Peak to the west, and of Yellowstone's peaks to the south. Backtrack on Soldier Creek Trail and northeast on Willow Way for the return.

The guests' favorite route—and the one with the best powder snow—is the intermediate Skully Loop. Skiers leave the Nordic tent heading north on Ezra, which quickly turns west and then south to inter-sect with the trails to Skully. Skiers climb to 7,600 feet and pass the ranch sawmill, a warming hut, and trails to Mountain Lion Run. There are views north toward Paradise Valley, the 10,921-foot Emigrant Peak, and the Crazy Mountains.

A don't-miss ranch favorite is skijoring behind the cattle boss and his horse. Skiers hang onto a waterski rope attached to the saddle. The steed walks, trots, or gallops around the skijoring course. There are also ski jumps to provide high-speed action for daring skiers and spectators.

There are other ski trails in the area, notably the Bear Creek Winter Trails system near Jardine, close to the north entrance to Yellowstone National Park. Bear Creek is a shared-use, U.S. Forest Service trail system frequented by snowmobilers. The trailhead at 6,500 feet accesses thir-teen loops, including the scenic Bear Fork Road that climbs to 8,400 feet.

Directions at a glance

From the parking lot near the A-frame and grizzly statue, look for the ivory-colored Nordic tent. Purchase a trail pass. Trails leave heading southwest, west, or north from the tent.

Some trails are packed, some are groomed, and three loops are track-set as needed. Maps and information are available from the Gardiner Ranger District.

How to get there

From Bozeman drive (locals suggest 4-wheel drive) or take the 4x4 Stage east 26 miles on Interstate 90 to Livingston. Exit at Highway 89 and drive 36 miles south. Turn west on Tom Miner Creek Road near mile marker 17. Cross the Yellowstone River on Carbella Bridge and turn left at the T. Drive 7.5 miles to the B Bar Ranch entrance, turn right into the ranch and drive 1 mile to ranch headquarters.

Red Lodge Area Trails
Red Lodge, Montana

Type of trail: ⬛ 🏵 ◀

Also used by: Elk, moose

Distance: 15 miles/25 kilometers

Terrain: Meadows, hilly

Trail difficulty: Easiest to more difficult

Surface quality: Machine-groomed and skier-set

Elevation: 5,670 to 7,200 feet

Food and facilities: Red Lodge Nordic Area yurt has outhouses, snacks, rentals, and lessons. Sylvan Peak in Red Lodge has maps and trail information and rents and sells ski and snowshoe gear. The Lake Fork Ski Trail's outhouse is at the western side of Loop 2 at the summer trailhead. Silver Run Ski Trail has an outhouse and maps at the trailhead. Beartooth Mountain Guides offers backcountry guiding, trail information, backcountry gear, and maps. There are several good restaurants in Red Lodge, including the Pollard's wood-grilled fare, Bridge Creek Backcountry Kitchen, Bogart's, and Red Lodge Pizza Company. Locals go to PD McKinney's for breakfast. The Pollard Hotel, a magnificently remodeled, turn-of-the-century hotel, was a former hang-out for Liver-Eatin' Johnson, Wild Bill Hickok, and Calamity Jane. Other lodging ranges from plush bed-and-breakfast inns to chain hotels.

Phone numbers: Red Lodge Nordic (406) 446–9191 or (406) 749–5610. Beartooth Mountain Shop (406) 446–1957. Sylvan Peak (406) 446–1770 or (800) 425–0076. The Pollard Hotel (800) POL-LARD (765–5273). Red Lodge Central Reservations (800) 444–8977 or (877) REDLODGE (733–5634). Red Lodge Chamber of Commerce (888) 281-0625. Beartooth Ranger District (406) 446–2103. Avalanche advisory (406) 838–2341 or (406) 587–6981.

Red Lodge, named for the color of the Crow Indians' tipis, sits at the base of the Beartooth Mountains. In the late 1800s, miners came by the hundreds to dig coal for the Northern Pacific Railroad. By 1910 Carbon County led Montana in coal production. When the Great Depression quashed industry, illegal bootleg liquor, labeled as "syrup," was distilled in Red Lodge and sent to San Francisco and Chicago. The most scenic road in the country, the Beartooth Highway, opened in 1936, crawling

over Beartooth Pass from Red Lodge to Cooke City. The highway generally opens for summer-to-fall travel in late May, and entices telemarkers and alpine skiers to schuss north-facing steeps along the road.

Three separate trails systems in the Red Lodge area vary from the machine-groomed Red Lodge Nordic Area to the skier-set trails of Lake Fork and Silver Run. The Red Lodge Nordic Area's 15 kilometers of groomed trails cover several loops. From the trailhead ski north on the Learning Loop to access most trails. There are views of the Beartooths, the Pryor Mountains, Grizzly Peak, and Mt. Maurice.

The Meadows loop is a wide-open ski, popular on full-moon nights. Dogs and snowshoers are welcome on Meadows and Lazy W Loop, the eastern-most trail. From the Learning Loop, ski north to the Meadows and ski the loop in either direction. The trail loops past aspen trees and back to the Learning Loop. At a northern side intersection, skiers and snowshoers without dogs can opt to ski onto Powerline Plunge, Palisades Point, and Whitetail Woods.

The Lake Fork XC Ski Trail, located on the edge of the Absaroka-Beartooth Wilderness, consists of two loops totaling 7 kilometers. The drainage sits between the Hellroaring Plateau and the Silver Run Plateau. Park at the summer trailhead where the road ends, at an elevation of 7,200 feet. If the road is closed, there is alternate parking right after the turnoff from Highway 212 at 6,850 feet. The trails are designed to be skied counterclockwise from the trailhead. It's single-track through pine trees and along the Lake Fork of Rock Creek to Lion's Camp. If the road is snowed in near the highway, you can ski on the road up to the summer trailhead, turn left/south, cross a wooden stock bridge, and follow the trail down to the next, smaller foot bridge, or else ski on to Lion's Camp and across another bridge to the parking area for the entire 7 kilometers. Taking the trail over the middle foot bridge short-cuts the lower Loop 1, reducing the route to 2 kilometers. Skiers wanting to sample the wilderness should check with Beartooth Mountain Guides or Sylvan Peak for information. Expert skiers climb from Lake Fork, over Sundance Pass to the West Fork of Rock Creek, a 28-mile expedition with a 3,900-foot elevation gain. Avalanche conditions exist, and route-finding skills are necessary.

Silver Run Ski Trail heads west from the parking area with four loops totaling 13 kilometers and paralleling West Fork Road on which snowmobiles travel. The trail begins at 6,500 feet elevation, climbing gradually through a thick forest of lodgepole pines. Loop 1 is suitable for beginners. Loops 2, 3, and 4 are all accessed from Loop 1, and continue on gentle terrain, finally looping back at the trail's highest elevation of 6,800 feet.

How to get there

Red Lodge Nordic Center is .75 mile from the junction of Highways 212 and 78. Drive Highway 78 north toward Columbus 1 mile and turn west on Fox Lane. Drive 1.75 mile. Look for the yurt on the north side and park along the road.

Silver Run is 5 miles southwest of Red Lodge. Drive 3 miles on West Fork Road #71, turn left/south at the first bridge onto Silver Run Road #2476, and park on the south side of the creek.

Lake Fork Ski Trail is just off Beartooth Highway 212, 10 miles south of town on the west side of the highway. Look for the Lake Fork road sign. Park in the parking areas just off the highway or drive in to the summer trailhead if the gate is open.

Directions at a glance

From the trailheads, the Red Lodge Nordic Area trails begin at the yurt in three directions, and the Silver Run and Lake Fork trails head west.

Cooke City/Kersey Lake/Rock Island Lake

Cooke City, Montana

Type of trail: ▬▬▬ ⬭

Also used by: Snowmobiles

Distance round trip: 10 miles/16 kilometers (from Cooke City)

Terrain: Flats and rolling hills

Trail difficulty: Easy to moderate

Surface quality: Snowmobile-packed, skier-packed, and backcountry

Elevation: 8,036 to 8,166 feet

Food and facilities: Cooke City offers accommodations and facilities, although the town caters more to snowmobilers than skiers. For ski gear, trail information, and shuttles to trailheads via snowmobile, contact the Cooke City Bike Shack. Only a handful of motels and cabins are open in winter so visitors should call the Chamber of Commerce for referrals. Big Bear Lodge Bed & Breakfast, located near the trailhead, shuttles guests via snowmobile from town. Avalanche transceivers are available for rent at several outlets, including Cooke City Bike Shack. Locals suggest the Miners Saloon and Emporium for pizza, and the Pine Tree Cafe for coffee, good food, and hanging out with the locals.

Phone numbers: Cooke City Bike Shack (406) 838–2412. Cooke City Chamber of Commerce (406) 838–2495. Big Bear Lodge Bed & Breakfast (406) 838–2267. High Country Motel (406) 838–2272. Avalanche information (406) 838–2341 or (406) 587–6981.

The ski trail to Kersey Lake and then to Rock Island Lake presents picturesque backdrops, a gentle backcountry experience, and the opportunity to ski into the Absaroka-Beartooth Wilderness, north and east of Yellowstone National Park. The Beartooth Mountains, with peaks over 12,000 feet, are the highest of Montana's mountain ranges. Among the Beartooths is the state's giant, Granite Peak, at 12,799 feet. Hundreds of glaciated alpine and subalpine lakes sit among the granite peaks. The beautiful Absaroka Range to the north is named for the Crow Indian word for crow. The 944,748 acres of the Absaroka-Beartooth Wilderness gained its official wilderness status in 1975. Watch for wolves, moose, mule deer, mountain goats, and bighorn sheep in this region.

Although the trailhead is only 3 miles from Cooke City on a summer road, it's a good idea to arrange a snowmobile shuttle to the trailhead to avoid high-speed snowmobile traffic. However, skiers can take the road,

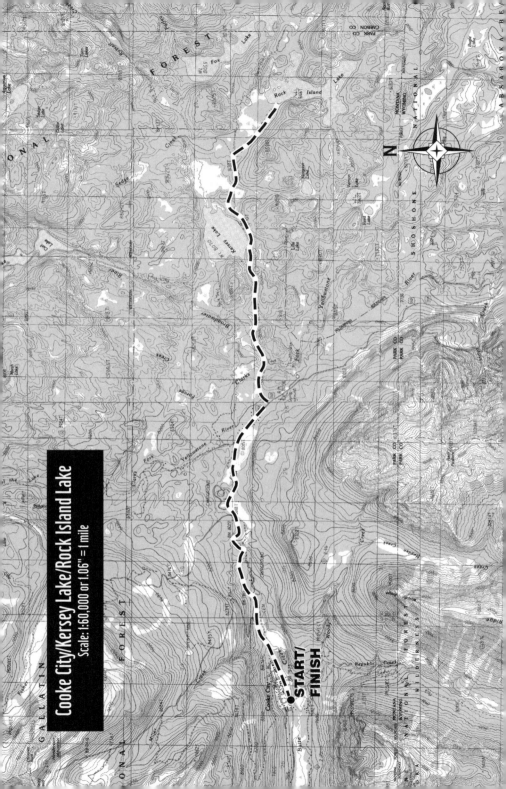

Cooke City/Kersey Lake/Rock Island Lake
Scale: 1:60,000 or 1.06" = 1 mile

START/
FINISH

Highway 212, climbing for 3 miles to the trailhead on the left/northeast. From the Kersey Lake horse/jeep trailhead, ski east .5 mile and meet up with foot trail. Follow the orange snowmobile trail markers on the trees. The route ventures east on a dual-use trail and equestrian access. Watch out for snowmobiles! The first landmark, located within 200 yards of the road, is a beautiful red barn, the property of Skyline Guide Service.

Follow the snowmobile tracks that lead to the north side of the barn and continue through meadows with short climbs up and down creek banks. At .5 mile there's a section where the trail branches. Take the foot/ski trail right/east off the snowmobile trail. Check your map to find a foot trail in the trees. The Kersey Creek drainage is visible from here. The snowmobile trail branches off left/north and goes through a burned area. The ski trail heads .5 mile through lodgepole pine and spruce up a draw to the Kersey Lake outlet. Ski past a Forest Service cabin hidden among trees on the west side of the stream, near the outlet of the lake. Snowmobilers generally do not use this trail because it is not groomed. A few ice fishermen may snowmobile in to Kersey Lake.

The southeast side of the lake is in the Absaroka-Beartooth Wilder-

Directions at a glance

From the parking area, ski north a block to the highway/snowmobile trail, then ski east (or take a snowmobile shuttle) on Highway 212 for 3 miles to the Kersey Lake trailhead. The trail leads left/northeast off the road. Look for the red barn to the left/north and the trail marker sign. If you come to the Chief Joseph Campground, you've gone too far.

ness and snowmobilers are not allowed here. To ski on to Rock Island Lake, ski the south/southeast shore of Kersey around the shoreline. There is a hiking trail that climbs up and over the ridge between the lakes; however, the best route is to ski around the ridge. At the large meadows at the head of the lake, head east and then southeast for a mile, going around a bluff above the lake and then right/east. At the next meadow, head southeast about .75 mile to Rock Island Lake. If you are winter camping at the lake, note that there are neither open facilities nor running water. Return to the trailhead on the same route.

How to get there

The only road to Cooke City that is open in winter is from Gardiner, Montana—the northern entrance to Yellowstone National Park. From Gardiner, drive south on Highway 89, the North Entrance Road, 5 miles to Mammoth. Turn left/east on Highway 212 and drive 52 miles to Cooke City. Watch for wildlife and especially wolves along this road. Once in Cooke City, park in the overnight parking area at the county dump. From the main street (Highway 212), turn right/south on Republic Street, and drive south 200 yards to the plowed parking area. Do not park on the street: Cars will either be plowed in or towed away.

About the Author

Jean Arthur is a writer and photographer who has written extensively on skiing and outdoor adventures. Her works have appeared in national magazines and newspapers, including *Smithsonian, Outside, Odyssey,* and *Backcountry.* Her first book, *Hellroaring: Fifty Years on the Big Mountain,* won an international award for excellence in ski history writing.

Jean describes herself as "a downhill skier gone bad." The great-granddaughter of Montana homesteaders, she learned to alpine ski at age four, began cross-country skiing and snowshoeing in college, and today skis several times a week during the season. She says, "I still love the gravity and speed of alpine skiing, but I find solace, fitness, and fun on the kick-and-glide trails."

A full-time writer, Jean makes her home in Whitefish, Montana, where both her daughters have been on cross-country skis since age two.

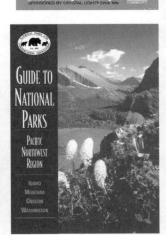